Critical Reasoning in Ethics

A lively and lucidly written text which students of applied ethics will find helpful. The author's liberal use of exercises as an aid to analysis is a notable feature, and to be commended.

David S. Oderberg, University of Reading

By demonstrating how specific logical skills apply to significant ethical problems and approaches, Anne Thomson effectively develops an extensive array of critical thinking skills interwoven with a solid introduction to ethical issues and views.
Charles Ess, Drury College, USA

For all those who wish to think clearly and informatively about ethics, this book should be read.
Nick Buttle, University of the West of England

Critical Reasoning in Ethics: A practical introduction offers a step by step introduction to the skills required for clear and independent thinking about ethical issues. Students are introduced to the three most important aspects of critical reasoning:

- how to understand and evaluate arguments;
- how to make well-reasoned decisions; and
- how to be fair-minded.

Anne Thomson builds on the highly successful *Critical Reasoning* to offer students the opportunity to practice their skills on real-life examples of ethical issues. Exercises at the end of each chapter include debates on abortion, animal rights, capital punishment, war and euthanasia and encourage the reader to identify arguments, conclusions and unstated assumptions, appraise evidence and analyse concepts, words and phrases.

Critical Reasoning in Ethics: A practical introduction deepens our understanding of the nature and role of moral concepts and assumes no prior knowledge of philosophy. It will be of interest to students taking courses in such disciplines as critical thinking, philosophy, politics, social work, social policy, nursing and the health professions as well as anyone who has to face moral dilemmas in a personal or professional context.

Anne Thomson is part-time lecturer in Philosophy and a Fellow of the School of Economic and Social Studies at the University of East Anglia. She is the author of the acclaimed *Critical Reasoning: A Practical Introduction*, also published by Routledge.

Critical Reasoning in Ethics

A practical introduction

■ Anne Thomson

Routledge
Taylor & Francis Group

LONDON AND NEW YORK

First published 1999
by Routledge
2 Park Square, Milton Park, Abingdon, Oxon OX14 4RN

Simultaneously published in the USA and Canada
by Routledge
711 Madison Avenue, New York, NY 10017

Routledge is an imprint of the Taylor & Francis Group, an informa business

© 1999 Anne Thomson

Typeset in Times by Routledge

British Library Cataloguing in Publication Data
A catalogue record for this book is available from the British Library

Library of Congress Cataloging in Publication Data
Critical reasoning in ethics: a practical introduction/Anne Thomson.
Includes bibliographical references and index. 1. Ethics. 2. Social
ethics. 3. Logic. 4. Reasoning. 5. Critical thinking. I. Title.
BJ43.T47 1999
98–31830
170–dc21
CIP

ISBN 13: 978-0-415-17184-7 (cased)
ISBN 13: 978-0-415-17185-4 (limp)

Contents

Acknowledgements

I am grateful to the *Independent* and the *Guardian* for granting me permission to use various articles which have been published in those newspapers.

I should like to thank also Edwina Currie for permission to quote her article, which appears in Chapter 3, on the age of consent for homosexuals; and Pat Walsh of the Centre of Medical Law and Ethics, King's College London for permission to quote her article, in Chapter 7, concerning religion and the right to life.

The extract from Judith Jarvis Thomson's 'A Defense of Abortion', which first appeared in *Philosophy and Public Affairs*, 1 (1971) is published by kind permission of Princeton University Press.

Thanks are due also to Nicholas Everitt, whose comments on the material in this book have been helpful; to students for stimulating discussions on the topics covered in the book; and to my family – Andrew, Mark and Neil.

Introduction

Everyone is faced with having to make decisions on ethical issues, – perhaps in personal relationships, such as whether to keep a promise to a friend, whether to terminate a pregnancy – or perhaps during the course of their work, such as whether to report a colleague's dishonesty, or how to treat clients or customers. There are other ethical issues on which the individual citizen's opinion may not have a direct impact – for example, whether capital punishment should be used, whether the country should intervene in wars, or the extent to which the country should give aid to less wealthy countries. Yet even on these more political issues, it is important that we have well-founded opinions, so that we can protest when those who do make the decisions – the politicians – seem to be in error.

What each of us needs in order to deal with ethical dilemmas is not a set of answers provided by someone else, but a set of skills to enable us to arrive at answers and make decisions for ourselves. This is important, partly because it enables us to take greater control of our lives, and partly because we do not yet know all the ethical questions which are likely to face us. Indeed, some quite new ethical questions can arise due to advances in science and technology – for example, the topical question as to whether it would be wrong to clone human beings. We need to be able to think clearly and to reason well about ethical issues.

Thus the aim of this book is not to offer solutions to a set of ethical dilemmas, but to encourage readers to do the thinking for themselves about these issues. It draws on ideas from the academic discipline of critical thinking, which has been defined in the following ways: 'To be a critical thinker is to be appropriately moved by reasons' (Siegel, 1988), and 'Critical thinking is skilled and active interpretation and evaluation of observations and communications, information and argumentation' (Fisher and Scriven, 1997). The emphasis in both these quotations is upon reasoning well, and the first definition suggests a link between reasoning well and acting appropriately.

Underlying this text are three important aspects of critical thinking – the ability to understand and evaluate arguments, the ability to make well-reasoned decisions, and the tendency to be fair-minded. Certain distinct skills are involved in the assessment of arguments and in good decision-making; for example, recognising reasons, conclusions and unstated assumptions, drawing conclusions, appraising evidence, evaluating statements and principles, and analysing words, phrases and concepts. The book offers practice in these reasoning skills, so that the skills can be both applied to topics within the text, and also carried over to topics not included in the book. Passages of reasoning (for the most part, extracts from newspapers) on a range of ethical issues are presented for illustration of the skills and for analysis. These issues include topics in the area of medicine, matters of life and death such as euthanasia and capital punishment, and questions as diverse as whether religion should be taught in schools and whether boxing should be banned.

Chapters 1, 2 and 3 deal with the analysis and assessment of moral reasoning. Chapter 4 presents and applies a model of decision-making. Chapter 5 offers practice in analysing moral concepts, and Chapter 6 introduces two moral theories as examples of principles which we need to evaluate. Chapter 7 concerns analysis and application of the idea of fair-mindedness. Each chapter includes exercises. Comments on some of the exercises in Chapters 1 and 2 are provided in Appendix 1. This will enable readers to check their progress in improving the skills of argument analysis and assessment. Appendix 2 provides summaries of the issues, concepts and arguments surrounding certain much debated ethical issues, namely abortion, euthanasia, the treatment of animals, environmental issues, capital punishment and war. These topics occur in examples and exercises throughout the book, so that readers will already have done some reasoning about them before they approach Appendix 2. The summaries, which bring together the relevant arguments, will encourage readers to deal with these topics in greater depth, and will enable them to devise their own well-reasoned arguments in response to the questions in Exercise 10.

Below is a summary of what readers can hope to achieve after working through the book.

- They should have improved their reasoning skills (such as identifying and evaluating reasons, conclusions, assumptions, analogies, concepts and principles), and their ability to use these skills in assessing other people's arguments, making decisions and constructing their own reasoning.
- They should develop an understanding of the role of certain moral concepts, principles and ethical theories in the discussion of ethical issues.
- They should have deepened their understanding of the debates on certain central issues in practical ethics, e.g. abortion, euthanasia, the treatment of animals, war and capital punishment.
- They may have strengthened certain valuable tendencies in themselves – to reason, to question their own reasoning and to be fair-minded.

Chapter 1

Analysing moral reasoning

Reasoning about moral or ethical issues such as abortion or euthanasia is often to be found in newspaper articles and letters to the editor. Those writing the articles may hold a particular point of view – for example that abortion is morally wrong – and wish to convince others that this point of view is right. One way to attempt to do this is to offer reasons or evidence which they believe supports their position: that is to say, they present an **argument**. What we mean by 'argument' in this context is a **reason** or a series of **reasons** which aim to support a particular claim, which is called the **conclusion**.

This is not the only context in which reasoning about ethics occurs. Sometimes we attempt to reason for ourselves about a particular ethical issue. For example, you may see a fellow worker stealing something from your employer, and experience a genuine dilemma as to what to do in these circumstances, since you feel some loyalty to your friend but also have a sense of responsibility to your employer. If the question you ask yourself is not 'What shall I do?', but 'What ought I to do', then you may engage in moral reasoning by considering the consequences of various courses of action, or by weighing the conflicting responsibilities, and attempting to come to a conclusion on the issue.

We have mentioned two instances of moral reasoning – written arguments (often in newspapers, but also to be found in textbooks, magazines, political pamphlets and so on), and the mental exercise of figuring something out for oneself. In this chapter we shall concentrate on written moral arguments, in order to help you to develop skills both in recognising when other people are presenting moral arguments, and in understanding the way in which someone's argument aims to support its conclusion. Chapters 2 and 3 will deal with assessment of moral arguments, and in Chapter 4 we shall offer practice in doing the reasoning for yourself on a number of ethical issues, when we introduce decision making.

Recognising moral arguments

In order to be able to recognise moral arguments, we need to be clear about two things:

(i)   What is the difference between an argument and a written passage which does not contain an argument?

(ii) What is the difference between a moral argument and a non-moral argument?

Let us consider the first of these.

Recognising arguments

All arguments, whether on ethical issues or not, will contain a main conclusion and a reason or reasons which are offered in support of the conclusion. Certain characteristic words – which we can call conclusion indicators – may be used to introduce a conclusion – for example, 'so', 'therefore', 'thus', 'hence' – as illustrated in the following passage:

> Most manufactured baby milks have been found to contain chemicals which can cause infertility. So mothers of new-born babies should be advised to breast-feed their babies.

Here the conclusion is the second sentence, and is introduced by 'So'. Where such words are used they can give us a clue that an argument is being presented, but we need to remember that these conclusion indicators also have other uses in language, so we cannot take it for granted that any passage which contains such a word must be presenting an argument.

There are a number of words which can function as reason indicators, which can also suggest to us that reasoning is taking place. Examples are 'because', 'for', and 'since'. The above argument could have read as follows:

> Mothers of new-born babies should be advised to breast-feed their babies, because most manufactured baby milks have been found to contain chemicals which can cause infertility.

In this example, the word 'because' signals that 'most manufactured baby milks have been found to contain chemicals which can cause infertility' is being offered as a reason for the conclusion that 'mothers of new-born babies should be advised to breast-feed their babies'.

Conclusions and reasons are sometimes introduced explicitly by a phrase which makes the author's intention very clear, for example 'it follows that', 'I draw the conclusion that', 'the reason for this is'. Other words which can indicate the presence of a conclusion are 'must' and 'cannot', as shown in the following two examples:

> He must have committed the murder. No-one else had the opportunity to do it, and his fingerprints were found on the murder weapon.

> People who accept that it is sometimes right to go to war cannot really believe that killing is always wrong. War inevitably involves killing.

In the first example the evidence presented in the second sentence is being used to support the conclusion that 'He *must* have committed the murder'. The second passage relies on the claim that war inevitably involves killing, in order to support the conclusion that those who are not in principle opposed to war *cannot* believe that killing is always wrong.

Although we can often find 'argument indicator' words to help us to identify arguments, it is possible for a passage to be an argument even if it contains no such words. Here is an example:

> Being aware of the dangers of driving too fast is not sufficient to stop people from speeding. Many drivers are still exceeding speed limits. A recent television campaign has emphasised the dangers of driving too fast, by showing home videos of children who were subsequently killed by speeding motorists.

In order to recognise this passage as an argument, we need to consider the relationships between the statements in the passage. Can any of the statements be taken to support any other statement? We could answer this question by considering each statement in turn, and asking 'Is any support or evidence given for this?' When we consider the first statement in this passage, we find that the rest of the passage can be taken to support the claim that awareness of the dangers of driving too fast does not stop drivers from speeding. The two further claims made in the passage – that many drivers are still speeding, and that there has been publicity about the dangers – are presented as reasons for accepting the conclusion expressed in the first sentence.

We have discussed two ways in which we might recognise an argument:

Remember

(i) by finding 'argument indicator' words (conclusion indicators, or reason indicators),

(ii) by finding a claim for which reasons appear to be offered.

If we have found 'argument indicator' words, then it is reasonable to assume that the writer was intending to present an argument. However, when we try to assess whether a written passage contains an argument, we are not simply trying to guess what the author's intentions were. A passage can function as an argument even if the author did not consciously set out to present an argument. It will function as an argument if it contains some claim (the conclusion) which is given support by other statements in the passage (the reasons).

There are many different purposes of written communication, and often, when, for example, we read newspaper articles, it will be obvious to us that an argument is *not* being presented. Some pieces of writing aim to tell a story, some to evoke our sympathy with a person's misfortune, some to amuse us, some to describe a scene, and some to present information to us without drawing any conclusions. However, the wording of a passage may sometimes mislead us into thinking that an argument is being offered, particularly when information is presented. For example, only one of the following two passages is an argument. Read them, and decide which one is an argument.

(a) Most mothers want the best for their babies. Some people think that it is better to feed babies on breast milk rather than on manufactured baby milks. Not all mothers find it convenient to breast feed.

(b) Mothers who go back to work soon after the birth of their babies find it inconvenient to breast feed. Trying to persuade such mothers to breast feed will only make them feel guilty. Instead, we should require employers to extend the period of paid maternity leave, so that mothers have more freedom of choice as to how to feed their babies.

In order to decide whether the passage is an argument, it is useful to ask first if there is a single main point which the passage is making. We can consider this question in relation to each of the statements in the passage. First passage (a) – does it try to convince us that most mothers want the best for their babies? It simply presents this as a piece of information, without giving us any evidence to support it. Does the passage try to convince us that some people think that it is better to feed babies on breast milk rather than on manufactured baby milks? Again, no support is given in the passage for this claim. Does it offer evidence for the claim that not all mothers find it convenient to breast feed? No, it simply presents this as a fact. There is a sense in which the passage aims to convince us of the truth of each of these statements, by presenting them as pieces of information, but not by presenting extra information or evidence which supports any of them. The statements are not interrelated in such a way that any one of them, or a combination of two of them, supports another. Hence this passage is not an argument, but simply presents information from which readers might draw their own conclusions.

Now let's consider passage (b). Does it support the claim that mothers who go back to work soon after the birth of their babies find it inconvenient to breast feed? No, it just tells us that this is so. Does it offer any evidence that trying to persuade such mothers to breast feed will only make them feel guilty? No, again, this is simply presented as a fact. Does it offer support for the claim that instead of trying to persuade these mothers to breast feed, we should require employers to extend the period of paid maternity leave, so that mothers have more freedom of choice as to how to feed their babies? The other two statements *do* appear to offer *some* reason for accepting this recommendation, in that the recommendation gives one possible solution to the problem identified by the other two statements – namely that there may be some mothers who want to breast feed their babies, and feel guilty about not doing so, but find it inconvenient to do so, because (perhaps for financial reasons) they go back to work. Thus it is reasonable to regard this passage as presenting an argument, though we may wish to question whether it is a very good argument. Perhaps the recommendation to require employers to extend maternity leave is unrealistic. Perhaps the argument relies on a questionable assumption – that it is better for babies to be breast fed than to be bottle fed. Perhaps there are other ways of solving the perceived problem – for example, convincing mothers that their babies can still be healthy if bottle fed, or providing crèches in places of employment, so that mothers can both work and take time off to breast feed their babies.

Examination of these two examples emphasises the fact that argument is not just a matter of presenting information. It is, rather, a matter of presenting a conclusion based on information or reasons.

Distinguishing moral from non-moral arguments

We now turn to the question as to what is distinctive about moral arguments. Does it really matter whether we can distinguish between a moral and a non-moral argument? In some respects, the two are alike, in that they present a reason or reasons for accepting a conclusion, and if we develop our skills in recognising arguments in general, then we are likely to be able to recognise moral arguments as arguments. Moreover, the basic steps we must take when we evaluate arguments (which will be set out in Chapter 2), are the same for both kinds of argument. However, the primary aim of this book is to improve reasoning skills applied to ethical issues, so it is important to learn to recognise those issues and features of language which suggest that a *moral* argument is being presented.

[margin note: Moral argument]

A moral argument, simply because it *is* an argument, will contain a conclusion, i.e. a claim in support of which some reasoning is offered. Think for a moment about what the idea of a moral or ethical claim involves. Before reading on, try to write down what you think are the important characteristics of a moral or ethical claim. You may find this very difficult, so perhaps as an easier first step, you could list a few examples of moral claims.

You may have come up with examples which claim that a certain action or activity or way of life is wrong – e.g. 'It is wrong to fiddle your tax return'. Or your examples may have been claims that someone, or everyone, ought or ought not to act in a particular way – e.g. 'Jamie should not hit other children'; 'Everyone ought to look after their elderly parents'; or 'Teachers should not use corporal punishment on pupils'.

[margin note: Moral arguments need a moral claim for a conclusion]

A moral argument must have a conclusion which makes some kind of moral claim, as do the examples quoted in the last paragraph. These moral claims are often expressed as recommendations, using the words 'should' or 'ought'. Even where they do not directly make a recommendation (e.g. 'It's wrong to fiddle your tax return'), it is clear that a recommendation is intended to follow from them ('So you shouldn't do it'). The words 'should', 'ought', 'right', 'wrong' can be described as evaluative terms, and they can indicate to us that a moral argument is being presented. Sometimes the evaluative aspect of a conclusion can be captured in an adjective – for example 'cruel', 'inhumane', 'admirable' and so on.

The presence of a recommendation or an evaluative term cannot be taken as a guarantee that a moral argument is being presented, since not all recommendations are moral recommendations, and not all evaluations are moral evaluations. Evaluative statements occur also in the context of aesthetic judgements, that is to say judgements as to what is beautiful in art, literature and music, or as to what is pleasing to other senses such as taste and smell. Recommendations can include such matters as what kind of car to buy or which career to pursue. We need to develop a sensitivity to evaluations which are moral as opposed to aesthetic or practical.

The distinction between moral and practical (sometimes referred to as 'prudential') recommendations can be made clear with some examples. For each of the following statements, decide whether it makes a moral or a prudential recommendation:

(i)   You want to live to a ripe old age, so you should take regular exercise.
(ii) You should look after your mother when she is ill.
(iii) No-one should drink and drive.
(iv) I want to get high grades, so I ought to attend lectures.
(v)   You should refrain from hitting your children.
(vi) If you want to keep a clean driving licence, you ought not to drink and drive.

The crucial difference between the moral and the practical recommendations lies not in the subject matter of these statements, but in the form or shape in which they are expressed. Numbers (i), (iv) and (vi) have the form 'You want *x*, so you should do *y*'. These are practical recommendations, addressed to those who have a particular interest or aim, and telling them what to do in order to achieve it. On the other hand, numbers (ii), (iii) and (v) do not specify any aim held by those to whom they are addressed. Their form is 'You should do *y*', and the implication is that you should do it regardless of what your aims and interests are. You should do it, because it is, quite simply, the right thing to do. These are examples of moral recommendations.

It will not always be obvious that a moral, as opposed to a practical recommendation is being made. Consider the following example:

> The Italians, who drink a lot of wine and eat a diet rich in fruit, vegetables and olive oil, have a lower incidence of heart disease than the British. The British government should therefore encourage its citizens to increase their consumption of wine, fruit, vegetables and olive oil, so that its citizens will be less susceptible to heart attacks.

Disregarding for the present the question as to whether this is a good argument, is it making a moral recommendation? There are two ways in which one could construe the second sentence. It could mean 'If the British government *wants* its citizens to be less susceptible to heart attacks, it should encourage them to consume more wine, fruit, vegetables and olive oil', in which case a merely practical recommendation is being made. Or it could mean 'The British government has a moral obligation to encourage its citizens to consume more wine, fruit, vegetables and olive oil, because this would make them less susceptible to heart attacks'. A thorough assessment of the argument would have to evaluate both of these two possible interpretations.

Another example in which it might be difficult to decide whether a moral argument is being offered is the argument presented on page 8:

> Mothers who go back to work soon after the birth of their babies find it inconvenient to breast feed. Trying to persuade such mothers to breast feed will only make them feel guilty. Instead, we should require employers to extend the period of paid maternity leave, so that mothers have more freedom of choice as to how to feed their babies.

Think for yourself about whether this is best understood as a moral argument.

Because making moral recommendations, either explicitly or implicitly, is central to moral arguments, it is tempting to define moral arguments as those arguments which tell us what is morally obligatory or what is morally forbidden. But this would exclude a whole class of arguments which defend claims that, contrary to what others may argue, something is neither morally obligatory, nor morally forbidden, but is morally permissible. For example, some people claim that abortion is morally wrong, from which it would follow that carrying out an abortion or seeking an abortion is morally forbidden. Someone arguing for the opposing view – that abortion is not morally wrong and is therefore morally permissible – is presenting a moral argument even though the conclusion does not make a claim about what is obligatory or forbidden. Such an argument aims to tell you what you *may* do, rather than what you should or should not do. Another example would be an argument with the conclusion that there is nothing morally wrong with being a conscientious objector when one's country is at war. This would be aiming to tell you that refusing to fight is morally permissible, contrary to claims that for males in a certain age group, fighting for one's country is morally obligatory. Of course, a huge amount of our normal everyday activity comes into the category of what is morally permissible, but we do not usually see any need to produce arguments to the effect that it is morally permissible to take out the rubbish or to mow the lawn. In general, arguments with conclusions that something is morally permissible will be on topics which are known to be contentious, and concerning which some of the disputants make claims that *x* or *y* is morally forbidden or morally obligatory.

Moral arguments, then, can come in a variety of guises. The use of certain words or phrases, or the discussion of certain issues, can alert us to the fact that a moral argument is being offered. Once we have satisfied ourselves that a moral claim is being made, we need to look in the text to see if reasons are given in support of it, in order to be sure that what is offered is argument, rather than dogmatic assertion of a point of view.

Exercise 1 Identifying moral arguments and conclusions

For each of the following, decide whether it is a moral argument, and, if it is an argument, identify the main conclusion. (NB some of these passages may not be arguments, and some may be arguments, but not moral arguments.)

Comments about each of these passages are made in Appendix 1.

1 Foxhunting and angling are similar in some respects. They are both done by human beings for their own enjoyment, and in both cases, an animal is made to suffer.

2 The fact that people disagree about moral matters is not a good reason for believing that there can be no rational discussion about morals. Scientists often disagree about scientific matters. This does not lead us to believe that there is no possibility of rational discussion between scientists.

3 A mouse is not a human being. Therefore there is no scientific justification for experimenting on mice in order to find out things about people.

4 It is argued, possibly with some justification, that skinny models provide unhealthy images for adolescents. But this does not mean that they should be criticised for presenting this image. No supermodel is chastised for smoking, a habit that is far more likely to kill her, and her admirers, than slimness. Nor do we persecute ballerinas, many of whom are not just anorexic, but crippled.

5 It is known that child molesters expose their victims to paedophiliac pornography to make sexual abuse seem normal. Likewise, certain films may have the effect of making violence acceptable to some children. Research has so far failed to assess the impact of such material.

(*Independent*, 26 November 1993)

---

6 Why should people who have been found guilty of supposed war crimes be punished? If it is because they have caused death and suffering, then surely that would mean that anyone who has killed another person in battle should be punished. Terrible things happen in wars, yet most people think that to fight in defence of one's country is not wrong. If war is morally justifiable, then killing the enemy during war-time cannot be wrong. And if it is not wrong, how can we say that those who perform such acts are committing a crime?

7 Some day soon we will have to ration energy use in planes and cars.... Here is one scheme some environmentalists have put forward. If as a nation we set a limit to the total number of air miles flown, or indeed to the number of car miles driven, we could issue a ration to every citizen. Those who did not want to use their driving or flying ration could sell their quota on the open market. The rich would scramble to buy, the poor to sell if they wanted to, if the price was enticing enough. Rations would become very valuable and it would lead to a healthy redistribution of wealth that had nothing to do with taxation. (Think what this principle could do for redistributing wealth between rich and poor nations too.)
(Polly Toynbee, *Independent*, 13 October 1997)

8 The idea that it is the fault of tobacco companies if smokers suffer from smoking related illnesses is crazy. We do not think that brewers are to blame for alcoholism, or that suppliers of dairy products are to blame for heart attacks and obesity. The tobacco companies are simply supplying a product which people can choose to buy or not to buy. The health risks of smoking are well known; warnings about the dangers even appear on the cigarette packets. It is tempting to look for someone to blame – and someone to sue – when misfortunes occur. But if anyone is to blame for a smoking related illness, it is the person who smokes in full knowledge of the risks.

9 Remission of prison sentences should not be based just on good behaviour, but on whether the prisoner is fit to rejoin society. If prisoners are considered a danger to the public they should not be let out when there are still some years of their sentence to run. So

rapists and arsonists should remain under lock and key until their sentence is completed.

10 The impression is created for the public that embryo research will bring treatment and miracle cures. That is cruelly untrue. Testing embryos for disorders and then destroying them offers no help to disabled people. Nor does it prevent handicap because it cannot stop new conditions arising in families with no previous history of them – a very common aspect of genetic disease.

Structure of arguments

Arguments can have a variety of structures. In order to be able to assess an argument, it is helpful first to work out its structure. Before we look in detail at the idea of structure, let us remind ourselves of the nature of argument – i.e. a reason or a set of reasons offered in support of a conclusion. Thus, there are two basic components of arguments – reasons and conclusions.

Reasons and conclusions

We have already learnt something about the nature of conclusions from examples of arguments given earlier. We know that a conclusion must make a claim. Another way of expressing this is to say that it must be presented as being true. We also know that a conclusion is sometimes, but not always, introduced by a 'conclusion indicator' word such as 'so' or 'therefore'. Looking back through previous examples will also show you that conclusions do not always appear at the end of arguments. They can occur at the beginning, as shown in both examples on page 7, or in the middle of an argument, as shown in the passage below.

> Anyone who works hard can improve their exam grades. Kim cannot have worked hard this year. Her exam grades are just as bad as they were last year.

We have said little about reasons so far. Many different kinds of statements can function as reasons, for example, items of scientific evidence, statistics, general principles. What they have in common is that they are offered in support of a conclusion, and, like conclusions, they are presented as being true. Because arguments have to start somewhere, not all of the reasons in an argument can be given support *within that argument*. <u>Every argument must have at least one basic reason for which no support is offered</u>. The evaluation of arguments, which will be introduced in Chapter 2, requires us to assess whether such reasons are true. But for the present, we are concerned simply with working out the structure of an argument, as a preliminary to evaluating it, so we shall not worry about the truth of reasons in this chapter.

The reasons and conclusions in an argument can fit together in a number of ways, the simplest of which is where one reason supports a conclusion. We have already seen some arguments with this structure, for example:

> People who accept that it is sometimes right to go to war cannot really believe that killing is always wrong. War inevitably involves killing.

Here we have:

> Reason: War inevitably involves killing.

offered in support of

> Conclusion: People who accept that it is sometimes right to go to war cannot really believe that killing is always wrong.

Another example of this simple structure is given below:

> Since we are not under an obligation to give aid unless aid is likely to be effective in reducing starvation or malnutrition, we are not under an obligation to give aid to countries that make no effort to reduce the rate of population growth that will lead to catastrophe.
> (P. Singer, 'Famine, Affluence and Morality' in W. Aiken and H. LaFollette (eds.) *World Hunger and Moral Obligation*, Englewood Cliffs, NJ: Prentice Hall, 1977, p. 35)

In this example we find a reason indicator, 'since', which tells us that the first part of the passage is a reason. The structure is as follows:

> Reason: We are not under an obligation to give aid unless aid is likely to be effective in reducing starvation or malnutrition.

offered in support of

> Conclusion: We are not under an obligation to give aid to countries that

make no effort to reduce the rate of population growth that will lead to catastrophe.

Sometimes two or more reasons are offered which, taken together, give support to the conclusion. This happens in the following example:

> Withholding information is just the same as lying. Lying is wrong. So withholding information is wrong.
> (T. Govier, *A Practical Study of Argument*, Belmont, CA: Wadsworth Publishing Company, 1985, p. 139)

You will have noticed that this argument contains the conclusion indicator 'So'. The structure can be set out as follows:

> Reason 1: Withholding information is just the same as lying.

> Reason 2: Lying is wrong.

presented together to support:

> Conclusion: So withholding information is wrong.

Both reasons are needed to support the conclusion. Although this example has only two reasons, it is possible for arguments to offer more than two reasons as jointly supporting a conclusion. However, sometimes when there are two (or more) reasons, they are offered not as jointly supporting the conclusion, but as independently supporting it, for example:

> Cigarette advertising should be banned because it encourages young people to start smoking. But even if it had no such influence on young people, it should be banned because it gives existing smokers the mistaken impression that their habit is socially acceptable.

The presenter of this argument clearly believes that each reason *on its own* is sufficient to support the conclusion that cigarette advertising should be banned, and would claim that the argument had established its conclusion if it could be shown *either* that cigarette advertising encourages young people to start smoking, *or* that cigarette advertising gives smokers the impression that smoking is socially acceptable. By contrast, in arguments in which the reasons are offered *jointly* in support of the conclusion, *all* the reasons must be true in order for the argument to be a good argument.

It may not always be clear whether the reasons are intended to support the conclusion jointly or independently, as, for example, in the following argument, first shown on page 7:

> He must have committed the murder. No-one else had the opportunity to do it, and his fingerprints were found on the murder weapon.

Perhaps the author regards each piece of evidence as sufficient in itself to show that 'he must have committed the murder'. However, taken together, the two pieces of evidence present a much stronger case, particularly since the presence of the suspect's fingerprints on the murder weapon may be explicable in some other way. Often an argument like this will be stronger if it presents joint rather than independent reasons for its conclusion, provided its reasons are all true.

Sometimes arguments present reasons for a conclusion which is then used, either on its own or with other reasons, to support a further conclusion. We can distinguish, then, between an **intermediate conclusion** and a **main conclusion**. This can be seen in the following example:

> It is clear that we have criteria for deciding whether people would make good parents, because couples who want to adopt children have to be assessed as to their suitability for parenthood. Since those people who do not satisfy the criteria for being good parents should not be allowed to become parents, no couples should be allowed to have a baby unless they have been granted a licence for parenthood.

There are two reason indicators in this passage – 'because' and 'since'. In the first sentence, 'because' indicates that a conclusion is being drawn, i.e. 'It is clear that we have criteria for deciding whether people would make good parents'. What the passage is ultimately trying to get us to accept – its main conclusion – is that 'no couples should be allowed to have a baby unless they have been granted a licence for parenthood'. The conclusion in the first sentence is an intermediate conclusion, and the argument can be set out as follows:

> Reason 1: Couples who want to adopt children have to be assessed as to their suitability for parenthood.

which is intended to support:

> Intermediate conclusion: It is clear that we have criteria for deciding whether people would make good parents.

This intermediate conclusion is taken together with:

> Reason 2: Those people who do not satisfy the criteria for being good parents should not be allowed to become parents.

in order to support:

> Main conclusion: No couples should be allowed to have a baby unless they have been granted a licence for parenthood.

This is just one example of an argument with a more complex structure, but arguments can become much more complicated than this, and their main conclusion may not appear at the end, as it does in this passage. However, the same steps are required regardless of how long and complex an argument is. They are summarised below.

Summary

1   Look for 'conclusion indicator' words, i.e. words such as 'so'. 'therefore', 'must', 'cannot', 'should'.

2   Look for 'reason indicator' words, i.e. words such as 'because', 'since'.

3   If there are neither 'conclusion indicator' nor 'reason indicator' words, look at each sentence in turn and ask, 'Does the rest of the passage give any extra information which tells me why I should believe this?' If the answer is 'No', then this sentence is not a conclusion. If the answer is 'Yes', then the sentence is a conclusion.

4   If none of the sentences in a passage is a conclusion, then the passage is not an argument. If at least one of the sentences in a passage is a conclusion supported by a reason or reasons in the rest of the passage, then the passage is an argument.

5   When you have found a conclusion in a passage, it may help you to rewrite the passage with the conclusion at the end, introduced by 'So'. Read through this re-written passage to check that it makes sense. If it does, then you can be confident that this passage is an argument.

6   Look for reasons and intermediate conclusions in your rewritten passage. Think about the way in which the reasons fit together, and try to write out the argument in the appropriate order of progression from basic reasons via intermediate conclusions to the main conclusion.

Do not worry at this stage about whether the reasons are true, or about whether they give conclusive support to the conclusion.

Unstated assumptions

Often those presenting arguments do not bother to state every single step in the argument. Careful analysis of the argument can show that something is being taken for granted, an assumption is being made which the author has not made explicit. But, of course, because the assumption is not stated, this can make the argument more difficult to analyse, so we need to develop the habit of looking for unstated assumptions.

All arguments will rely on numerous assumptions in the form of a body of background knowledge and shared beliefs and meanings. Although many of these assumptions will be uncontentious, sometimes an argument rests upon a dubious assumption which we must make explicit in order to evaluate the argument.

We are going to look at examples of unstated assumptions of two kinds, those which underlie a basic reason of the argument, and those which function as a missing step within the argument, either as a missing additional reason which must be added to the stated reasons in order for the conclusion to be established, or as a missing intermediate conclusion which is supported by the reasons and in turn supports the main conclusion.

In our first example, it is possible to identify an assumption which underlies a basic reason presented in the argument.

> Allowing parents to choose the sex of their children could have serious social costs. There would be a higher percentage of males who were unable to find a female partner. Also, since it is true that 90 per cent of violent crimes are committed by men, the number of violent crimes would rise.

There are two reasons given for the conclusion that allowing parents to choose the sex of their children could have serious social consequences. The reasons are that it would result in more males who could not find female partners, and it would lead to an increase in violent crime (since most violent crimes are committed by males). However, these two results would occur only if there was an increase in the male to female ratio in the population. So these two reasons rely on the assumption that if parents were allowed to choose the sex of their children, there would be a greater tendency to choose male offspring than to choose female offspring. The assumption can be stated as follows:

> If parents were able to choose the sex of their children, there would be more parents who chose to have boys than parents who chose to have girls.

We have described this as an assumption underlying a basic reason, and as regards the first reason, this relationship is straightforward:

> Assumption: If parents were able to choose the sex of their children, there would be more parents who chose to have boys than parents who chose to have girls,

gives support to:

> Reason 1: There would be a higher percentage of males who were unable to find a female partner.

However, the third sentence of the passage can be seen to contain two distinct claims, and we can separate these into two reasons, one of which, together with the assumption, supports the other, as follows:

> Reason 2: 90 per cent of violent crimes are committed by men.

Taken together with:

> Assumption: If parents were able to choose the sex of their children, there would be more parents who chose to have boys than parents who chose to have girls,

gives support to:

> Reason 3 (or intermediate conclusion): The number of violent crimes would rise.

Reason 1 and Reason 3 jointly give support to the main conclusion. Thus the assumption we have identified functions in two ways in this argument; first it underlies one of the basic reasons, and second, it functions as an additional reason, which, taken together with another basic reason, supports an intermediate conclusion.

The assumption may be true, but, without further evidence, we cannot be certain that it is. Identifying the unstated assumption helps us to see exactly what claims we must assess in order to evaluate the argument.

Now let us look at an example in which an assumption functions simply as an additional reason within the argument.

> For a victim of rape, appearing in court is a very distressing experience. If the defendant pleads guilty in a rape case, the victim does not have to

appear in court. So, in such cases, sentences should be lighter for those who plead guilty than for those who plead not guilty.

Before reading on, think about the reasoning in this passage. What needs to be added to the two reasons which have been stated, in order to give support to the conclusion?

It is clear that the passage is trying to get us to accept that in rape cases, sentences should be lighter for those who plead guilty than for those who plead not guilty. The reasons it offers for this are that when the defendant in such a case pleads guilty, the victim does not have to appear in court, and appearing in court is very distressing for the victim. What bearing do these statements have on the conclusion? The recommendation made in the conclusion is aimed at reducing the likelihood that victims will have to appear in court. How would reducing sentences for those who plead guilty achieve this? It would do so if reduced sentences made defendants more likely to plead guilty. It has not actually been stated in the passage that if sentences were lighter for those who plead guilty to rape, more defendants would do so, but it is assumed. We can set out the argument as follows:

> Reason 1: For a victim of rape, appearing in court is a very distressing experience,

and

> Reason 2: If the defendant pleads guilty in a rape case, the victim does not have to appear in court,

and

> Assumption: If sentences were lighter for those who plead guilty than for those who plead not guilty, defendants would be more likely to plead guilty.

These two reasons and the assumption jointly give support to:

> Conclusion: So, in such cases, sentences should be lighter for those who plead guilty than for those who plead not guilty.

You may question the truth of the assumption, and you may also think that even if it were true, this would not justify the recommendation for lighter sentences for the same crime.

Our final example has an assumption which functions as an intermediate conclusion. We first saw this passage on p. 7 as an example of an argument without argument indicator words.

> Being aware of the dangers of driving too fast is not sufficient to stop people from speeding. Many drivers are still exceeding speed limits. A recent television campaign has emphasised the dangers of driving too fast, by showing home videos of children who were subsequently killed by speeding motorists.

Can you spot a stage of the argument which has not actually been stated?

The conclusion of the argument is the first sentence. In order to convince us that knowing the dangers of driving too fast is not enough to stop people doing it, the passage points out that drivers are still speeding, even though there has been an advertising campaign on television drawing attention to the fatalities caused by speeding. However, those motorists who are speeding may not have seen the television campaign, or may not have believed that excessive speed was the cause of the deaths. So they may not know the dangers of speeding; but in order to draw its conclusion, the argument must assume that they do. It takes it for granted that because there has been the television campaign, all drivers have understood and accepted its message about the dangers of speeding. We can analyse the argument as follows:

> Reason 1: A recent television campaign has emphasised the dangers of driving too fast, by showing home videos of children who were subsequently killed by speeding motorists.

This gives support to:

> Assumption (intermediate conclusion): All motorists must know the dangers of driving too fast.

This assumption is taken together with:

> Reason 2: Many drivers are still exceeding speed limits,

to give support to:

> Main conclusion: Being aware of the dangers of driving too fast is not sufficient to stop people from speeding.

Looking at these examples has led us to question the truth of some of the assumptions we have identified, which shows us that a thorough analysis of an argument leads very naturally onto the next step of assessing the argument. However, before we go on to the details of assessment, we shall look at a few more features of reasoning.

Other devices in reasoning

Analogies or comparisons

Amongst the assumptions which can underlie someone's reasoning, we often find an assumption that two objects or two situations or two cases are comparable, so that whatever we can conclude in the one case, we are also entitled to conclude in the other case. Sometimes these analogies are quite explicit. For example, someone may claim that animals are like people, in that they can experience pain and they can form emotional attachments, so if we should not kill people, neither should we kill animals. In other cases, the explicit claim that x is like y may not be made, yet the reasoning offers the analogy on the assumption that the two are comparable. This happens in the following example.

Analogy - "a is like b"

> We shouldn't praise people for their intelligence. After all, we wouldn't think it was appropriate to praise someone for being six feet tall or having brown eyes, since individuals do not produce these characteristics in themselves by their own efforts.

In this passage there is no explicit statement that intelligence is like certain physical characteristics, but the point of mentioning the physical characteristics is to get us to see an analogy between them and intelligence. It is assumed that intelligence, height and eye colour are alike in that we are not responsible for producing these characteristics in ourselves.

The use of analogy can be a powerful tool in reasoning, because it can remind us of the need for consistency. If we accept that x is like y in all relevant respects, then we should accept that what we can conclude about x, we must also conclude about y. However, not all analogies are good analogies, because there may be important differences between the two things which are claimed to be analogous. For example, in relation to the claim about intelligence, we may agree that we are not responsible for producing our own level of intelligence, yet think that intelligence differs from the other characteristics mentioned, in that praising people for their intelligence may have some beneficial effects. Praising someone for being six feet tall will not make any difference to his height, but praising someone for his intelligence may give him an incentive to use his intelligence, for his own good and for the good of others.

Think about our other example for yourself. Do animals, like humans, experience pain and form emotional attachments? Are there any differences between humans and animals which could justify killing animals even though it is unjustifiable to kill humans?

We have examined the use of reasons in arguments, where the function of a reason is to support a conclusion. Another way of expressing this is to say that in an argument, someone is giving *reasons for* believing something to be true. This can be contrasted with giving *reasons why* something is as it is, in other words, *explaining* something which is already accepted as true.

Here is an example of an explanation:

> Statistics show that the population of Britain is increasing. This is because the average age at which people die has risen, due to improvements in diet and medicine.

Here the fact which is being explained is the increase in Britain's population, and the explanation seems a good one, both because it is easy to accept the truth of what is stated in the explanation, and because there is an obvious connection between the explanation and the fact which is being explained. We frequently hear that more people are surviving into old age, and given that this is true, there are likely to be increasing numbers of people who are alive and to be counted in a population census. The other factor which makes this seem a good explanation is that it is difficult to think of a plausible alternative explanation. Another influence on the size of the population is the birth rate, and if the birth rate were rising, then this could explain, or partially explain, the increase in the population. But we are frequently told that the birth rate is not rising. Of course, an increase in immigration could produce an increase in the population, so in order to be confident that the explanation offered is correct, we would need to refer to statistics on immigration.

It is sometimes difficult to judge whether someone is offering an argument or an explanation, since the same words which are used to introduce explanations (e.g. 'because' in our example above) are used in arguments to introduce reasons. For example, it would have been less clear that the above passage was an explanation if it had been worded as follows:

> The population of Britain is increasing because the average age at which people die has risen, due to improvements in diet and medicine.

One way to understand this reworded passage would be:

> Reason: The average age at which people die has risen, due to improvements in diet and medicine,

offering support for:

> Conclusion: The population of Britain is increasing.

However, it is a less natural reading of the passage, since usually if someone wanted to convince us that the population was increasing, they would refer to statistics showing an increase over the years, instead of taking the roundabout route of offering evidence about greater longevity. You will have to use your judgement in such cases. You need to ask, 'Is this passage offering reasons for accepting that a particular claim is true, or reasons why an accepted fact is as it is?'

Our example was of an explanation occurring as an independent piece of reasoning, but explanations can also appear as part of the reasoning in an argument. It is useful for our purposes to be aware of the role of explanations in reasoning, because an argument on an ethical issue could depend upon one or more explanations. What we need to know about explanations is whether they are the correct explanations of the facts or phenomena they seek to explain. Two strategies can help us to assess this. The first is to look for any questionable assumptions upon which the explanation relies. The second is to think of other possible explanations of the phenomenon. If there is more than one plausible explanation of a phenomenon, then it would be sensible to reserve judgement until we have more information.

More features of ethical arguments

The components of arguments – reasons, conclusions and assumptions – and the devices discussed in the last section – analogies and explanations – are common to reasoning both on ethical issues and on subjects with no ethical or moral implications. The features discussed in this section – concepts and principles – are also features of reasoning in general, but because they play a very important role in moral reasoning, we shall look at specific examples of the use of moral concepts and moral principles.

Moral concepts

A concept is an idea or a set of ideas associated with a particular word or phrase. For example, we could talk about the concept of freedom, or the concept of democracy. These words are probably difficult to define, because people have different understandings of what they mean, but if we want to use such terms in arguments, or if we wish to evaluate an argument containing such terms, we need a very clear idea of their implications. We could probably begin to say something about what these terms mean – for example 'Freedom means being able to do what you want' – but we may find that when we consider the implications of this simple definition, we need to modify it and aim for a deeper analysis of the meaning. We shall look at analysis of concepts in more detail in Chapter 5.

For the present, you need to look out for the use of concepts which may require deeper analysis, but we do not propose to present a list of all the moral concepts you are likely to meet. Instead, we shall present one or two examples of moral arguments, and pick out the moral concepts upon which they rely.

Here is an example of a short argument which relies upon a concept which is very commonly used in ethical arguments.

> A foetus' heart is beating by 25 days after fertilisation. Abortions are typically done 7 to 10 weeks after fertilisation. Even if there were any doubt about the fact that the life of each individual begins at fertilisation, abortion clearly destroys a living human being with a beating heart and a functioning brain. If the first right of a human being is his or her life, the direct killing of an unborn child is a manifest violation of that right.

This argument uses evidence about the stage of development which a foetus has reached at the time at which abortions are usually carried out in order to draw a conclusion that if human beings have a right to life, then abortion must be a violation of that right. The principal moral idea upon which this argument rests is the idea of a right to life. If we are to be able to evaluate this argument, we are going to have to understand what the idea of a right to life involves – what kinds of behaviour does it require or rule out, and what kinds of beings have a right to life. We shall leave detailed discussion of these issues to a later chapter.

Let us look at another example:

> The only excuse there could be for introducing a privacy law would be that it would reduce harm. But it would be wrong to have such a law. Although it would protect individuals from harm, in that it would deter the press from publishing details of their private lives, it would be used to suppress the publication of matters of genuine public interest. This would be much more harmful than allowing some individuals to suffer unwelcome intrusion by the press into their private lives.

This passage relies on the idea of 'harm' as an important moral consideration. In rejecting the call for a privacy law to protect individuals from intrusion by the press, it does not suggest that the harm such people might suffer is irrelevant. Rather it claims that greater harm would be caused by a privacy law than would be prevented by it. Many moral arguments rely on the concept of harm, and we shall need to be clear about what counts as harm, and whether some cases of harm are too trivial to be taken as moral considerations.

You are likely to meet other moral concepts in ethical arguments. Look out for important ideas upon which an argument seems to rely, and which you think need to be clarified or precisely pinned down.

Moral principles

Like a moral or value. 'Harm, Freedom,' not lie, cheat, steal"

A principle is a general rule or recommendation which applies to a number of specific cases. For example, a business may operate on the principle that excessive time should not be spent on making decisions, on the grounds that most decisions made fairly quickly will turn out to be profitable, and such profit will more than compensate for any losses made by an occasional over-hasty decision. Of course, this is not an example of a *moral* principle, but moral principles have the same characteristic of encompassing a number of individual cases. They may appear in arguments as very general statements which function as reasons; or they may underlie arguments as unstated assumptions.

Principles can be closely related to moral concepts. For example, the concept of a right to life which was used in the argument about abortion in the last section is very closely related to the principle that killing is wrong; the concept of harm used in the argument on privacy laws is related to the principle that we should avoid harming others.

These principles apply to many different cases, and in the next chapter we shall consider the way in which we can make some evaluation of a principle by identifying some of the cases to which it must apply. For the present, be alert to the use of principles in the arguments presented in the next set of exercises.

Exercise 2 Analysing moral arguments

In most of the passages we have analysed, each sentence of the text can be classified as a reason or a conclusion. In this exercise, some of the texts may include extra material, for example, background information, so you may need to pick out the components of the argument.

Analyse each of the following arguments by:

- identifying the main conclusion
- identifying the reasons
- identifying any assumptions and intermediate conclusions
- identifying any moral concepts
- identifying any moral principles
- identifying any analogies or explanations.

In Appendix 1, you will find comments about those arguments marked here with an asterisk.

1 [If killing an animal infringes its rights, then] never may we destroy, for our convenience, some of a litter of puppies, or open a score of oysters when nineteen would have sufficed, or light a candle in a summer evening for mere pleasure, lest some hapless moth should rush to an untimely end. Nay, we must not even take a walk, with the certainty of crushing many an insect in our path, unless for really important business! Surely all this is childish. In the absolute hopelessness of drawing a line anywhere, I conclude that man has an absolute right to inflict death on animals, without assigning any reason, provided that it be a painless death, but that any infliction of pain needs its special justification.

    · childish reasons

    ← conclusion

    ← assumption

(Lewis Carroll, 'Some Popular Fallacies About Vivisection', in *The Complete Works of Lewis Carroll*, Nonesuch, 1939, p. 1,072)

2* The use of cannabis should be made legal because it is no more harmful than other drugs – alcohol and tobacco – the use of which is legal. Since the purpose of laws is to protect us from harm, there is no point in having a law against the use of cannabis.

    conclusion

    ← Reason

    principle: Laws are for protecting us from harm

3 Here are two statements. 'If an animal is terminally ill and in severe pain, it is right to kill it painlessly to prevent further suffering'. 'It is wrong to kill a human being who is terminally ill and in severe

pain, even if the individual requests it'. People who think that both these statements are true must either have less compassion for human beings than for animals, or have less respect for the lives of animals than for the lives of human beings. Therefore, such people are being inconsistent.

4* Because adults see the modern world as a dangerous place, they tend to become over-protective towards children. They should resist this temptation, because it has the opposite effect to that which is desired. Children who are usually ferried around in cars have little chance to learn road safety for themselves, and may be in greater danger when they do have to cross a road. We must also remember that children need the freedom to make mistakes in order to learn about the dangers in the world.

5 Live animal experimentation should not be a case of out of sight out of mind, for two reasons. One is that some people – though not as many as the animal rightists like to claim – object passionately to all animal experiments. For their sake extensive public debate, and, if necessary, mobilisation of the majority view, are vital. The other is a more general reason, to do with living in a society dominated by expertise. Too often in the modern world we ignore what goes on behind the laboratory door.... The public applauds when scientists announce some great breakthrough. But the public does not engage with the researchers, scrutinising and seeking to understand the necessity of their work. We do not often enough ask whether deploying the utilitarian argument – that painful means are justified by less (human) pain in the end – always suffices.
(Leading article, *Independent*, 22 October 1997)

6* What should we do with the 3,300 frozen embryos due to perish on 1 August? The law says that these spare embryos, created for couples undergoing IVF treatment, should be destroyed after five years unless the couple want them preserved for a further five years. David Alton, the 'pro-life' MP, predictably takes a different view: he wants these 'orphans' to be put up for adoption....

Ideally each couple should now decide the future of those embryos.... But 900 couples cannot be traced. Perhaps the Human Fertilisation and Embryology Authority should make more effort to track them down and force them to make the decision themselves. But should they fail to do so, the procedures are clear; as the producers expect, the embryos should be destroyed.

The pro-life lobby believes that the rules are immoral. However, it would be far more unethical to change the rules now. Imagine if we took David Alton's advice. Couples could suddenly find that against their wishes someone else was bearing and bringing up the brother or sister of their own children. That wasn't something they were warned about when they first agreed to fertility treatment. Nor is it something they should be forced to deal with and adjust to now.

(Leading article, *Independent*, 24 July 1996)

7   A small frisson of unease swept through the pro-abortion lobbies yesterday. Was it possible, as a last desperate gesture, clutching at straws, that the Conservative Party might come out for a tightening of the abortion law? After all, it can be made to seem quite reasonable. As modern technology keeps foetuses alive at an earlier and earlier stage, so the legal date for abortion needs to be made earlier too.

It is an argument to be strenuously resisted. Who needs late abortions? The most hopeless, desperate cases, the 14-year-olds who have no idea what is happening to them, the very stupid and the mentally retarded: all the people who would make the worst mothers. And if soon foetuses can be kept alive at any stage, will we ban abortion altogether?

(Polly Toynbee, *Independent*, 1 January 1997)

8* Of crimes against the person, murder is in one clear sense unique, for it does not merely harm the victim, but deprives him of existence.... But many other crimes come very little way behind it: torture, rape, mutilation and severe bodily damage.

So how should we treat those convicted of such crimes? A crude answer would be that we should treat them as they have treated others: we should torture those who have tortured, rape those who have raped, mutilate those who have mutilated, and kill those who have killed; that would not be revenge, which seeks to inflict the greatest harm upon its object, but retribution.

Nobody maintains this in the first three of these cases; almost everyone can see that, if doing something is abhorrent, doing it in return is likewise abhorrent. The grisly apparatus of state executions, accompanied by the ghoulish relish exhibited by the less restrained members of the public, is no appropriate expression of our horror at the taking of a life. To reintroduce it would not testify to a renewed reverence for human life; it would witness to an increased callousness about destroying it.

(Michael Dummett, *Guardian*, 17 April 1995)

Chapter 2

Assessing moral reasoning

During our discussion in the last chapter of assumptions underlying arguments, we began to ask questions about whether the arguments were good ones – questions as to whether we should accept the conclusions which were presented. In this chapter we shall focus directly on the assessment of arguments, and we shall find that there are two crucial questions which we must ask when we assess any argument.

Let us approach these questions by considering two examples. In Chapter 1, we looked at the following argument:

> Withholding information is just the same as lying. Lying is wrong. So withholding information is wrong.
>
> (T. Govier, *A Practical Study of Argument*, Belmont, CA: Wadsworth Publishing Company, 1985)

The conclusion is that 'withholding information is wrong'. Does this argument succeed in establishing this conclusion? Before reading further, try to answer this question by writing down some objections to the argument.

Perhaps you commented that there may be some circumstances in which telling a lie is not the wrong thing to do – if, for example, it

prevents a tragedy. For example, suppose you knew that a Jewish family such as Anne Frank's family in Amsterdam were hiding from the Nazis, and you were asked about their whereabouts. Would it be wrong to say that you didn't know where they were, even if you did? This objection suggests that the first reason in the argument may be stated in too general a way, and thus may not be universally true. Or your objection may have been that withholding information is not the same as lying – for example, you may think that failing to tell someone your age is not the same as lying about your age. In that case you would be claiming that the second reason in the argument is not true. If these reasons are not true, why should we be required to accept a conclusion which follows from them? Of course, this is not the same as saying that the conclusion is false. Perhaps good reasons could be produced for accepting that, at least in some circumstances, withholding information is wrong. But when assessing an argument we want to know whether *these* reasons establish *this* conclusion, and if the reasons are not true then they cannot establish anything. In this example, we may not be prepared to state categorically that the reasons are false, but there is at least some doubt about their truth. This illustrates that one of the questions we must ask when assessing any argument is:

Are the reasons true?

Our second example, also first seen in Chapter 1, relates to the other question which is vital for assessment of an argument.

> For a victim of rape, appearing in court is a very distressing experience. If the defendant pleads guilty in a rape case, the victim does not have to appear in court. So, in such cases, sentences should be lighter for those who plead guilty than for those who plead not guilty.

The conclusion of this argument is clearly that in rape cases, sentences should be lighter for those who plead guilty than for those who plead not guilty. We pointed out earlier that the reasoning relies on an unstated assumption that if sentences were lighter for those who plead guilty in rape cases, more defendants would plead guilty – a questionable assumption since most defendants may not expect to be found guilty. Let us suppose that the reasons offered in this argument are true – that is to say that appearing in court is indeed distressing for rape victims, and that they would not have to do so if the defendant pleaded guilty. Let us also suppose that the assumption is true – i.e. that lighter sentences for those who plead guilty would lead to an increase in guilty pleas, and thus a reduction in the number of victims who must appear in court. Do these reasons give strong support to the conclusion?

They would certainly support a conclusion that making sentences lighter for defendants who plead guilty to rape would reduce the number of rape victims who suffered the distress of appearing in court. But in order to conclude that such a policy should be introduced, we would surely have to be satisfied that it would have no adverse effects, or that there were no better ways of achieving the aim of reducing distress for victims. Even rape victims themselves may object to convicted rapists getting shorter sentences simply because they had pleaded guilty. Perhaps the distress of giving evidence would be reduced if victims were allowed to give evidence on video, rather than having to sit in the same court as their attacker. So, even if the reasons and the assumption are true, they may not be sufficient to give strong support to the conclusion. This illustrates the importance of the second question we must ask when assessing any argument:

> Is the conclusion well supported by the reasons given for it?

In Chapter 1, we pointed out that arguments can have unstated assumptions which function in the same way as reasons, so it is important to assess whether unstated assumptions, as well as reasons, are true. Our analyses of the structure of arguments also showed that arguments can have intermediate conclusions, as well as a main conclusion, so it is important to assess whether intermediate conclusions are well supported. Our two vital questions for the assessment of arguments thus become:

> Are the reasons (and any unstated assumptions) true?

> Is the main conclusion (and any intermediate conclusion) well supported by the reasons given for it?

Can moral arguments be assessed?

Not everyone accepts that moral arguments can be assessed in the way set out above. Some philosophers have insisted that because of these requirements of assessment, together with two features of moral discourse, it is impossible to engage in reasoned argument about moral issues. Although it is not the central purpose of this book to explore the more theoretical aspects of argument analysis, it is important to lay to rest these worries about the possibility of ethical reasoning, all the more so since philosophers are not the only people who worry about this possibility. Many people think that we cannot reason about ethics, that we can only rely on our feelings about ethical issues. If this were so, then it would be pointless to attempt to assess whether arguments about such issues present a good case for a particular conclusion. Instead, we would only be interested in how we feel about the conclusion – the reasoning would be irrelevant.

Let us examine the two features of ethical discourse which threaten to undermine the possibility of ethical reasoning. They are commonly referred to as 'the fact/value distinction' and 'the is/ought gap'.

The fact/value distinction and the truth of reasons

The fact/value distinction rests upon the assumption that statements which we make about the world can be divided into those which are merely factual and those which are either partly or wholly evaluative. It is also assumed that factual statements can be true or false, whereas the concepts of truth and falsity are not applicable to evaluative statements. This is not the same as saying that we can easily find out whether factual statements are true, whereas it is difficult to find out whether evaluative statements are true. With some factual statements – for example, 'There is life outside our universe' – it may be very difficult to find out if they are true. But whether we can find out or not, the statement *is* either true or false. By contrast, evaluative statements, it is claimed, could not possibly have either the status of being true or the status of being false. So statements such as 'Vermeer's paintings are beautiful', 'Jellied eels taste disgusting', 'Stealing is wrong' cannot be judged to be either true or false. The first two of these statements are examples of aesthetic judgements – i.e. judgements about what is pleasing to the senses – and the view that such judgements are mere matters of individual taste (that 'Beauty is in the eye of the beholder') is widespread. Must we accept that moral evaluations are also mere matters of individual taste, and that statements such as 'Stealing is wrong', 'You shouldn't tell lies' cannot be assessed for truth or falsity?

The first objection to make here is that, even though many people say that moral evaluations are merely matters of opinion, hardly anyone behaves as if this were so, especially when trying to convince others of a moral point of view. If I say 'Euthanasia is wrong', and you disagree with me, you *may* reply 'That statement is neither true nor false – it's just that you happen to dislike the idea of euthanasia, and I don't'. But you are much more likely to try to give me reasons for thinking that in some circumstances, euthanasia is acceptable – for example when individuals with a painful terminal illness choose to have their intolerable suffering brought to an end. When we discussed earlier the argument which claimed that lying and withholding information were both wrong, we *questioned the truth* of the statement 'lying is wrong' by considering cases in which telling a lie could be the right thing to do. We didn't say 'This statement just isn't the sort of statement which could be either true or false'. And you probably did not think that there was anything odd about this approach, because most of us act as if moral evaluations are capable of truth or falsity.

A second, and related, objection concerns the assumption that moral evaluations are simply reflections of our feelings, rather than conclusions of our reasoning. This suggests that in order to settle what our moral position is, we should simply look into our hearts and consult our feelings. But for most of us there will be moral issues about which we do not yet have definite feelings. Consulting our feelings may not tell us whether, for example, we should become vegetarians or whether abortion is morally wrong. What we want to know is how we *should* feel about these issues, what are the *reasons* for thinking that having an abortion would be the right or the wrong thing to do. Moreover, suppose I looked into my heart and discovered that I was a racist. Would this be a good enough justification for treating members of other races badly?

Our third objection questions whether the distinction between factual and evaluative statements can be maintained. We are usually invited to see a contrast between a statement which in an unproblematic way refers to a fact in the world, and an evaluative statement which seems to add something non-factual to what could have been a purely factual statement. For example 'The cat is sitting on the mat' is a factual statement, and there is some state of affairs in the world – a cat and its whereabouts at a particular time – which determines whether the statement is true or false. But suppose we wish to make a true statement about the following situation. The children are sitting on the cat. We know they are hurting the cat; one of them utters shouts of glee as he bounces up and down on the animal; the other squashes the cat with a determined and malevolent expression on her face. How should we accurately describe this? If we were to say 'The children are being cruel to the cat', we would be making an evaluative statement, since 'cruel' carries the connotation that they are deliberately doing something they should not be doing, namely, hurting the cat. This may or may not be an accurate description. It would be untrue if the children did not know they were hurting the cat. But, assuming that they did know this, why should the evaluative statement be any less factual, and any less accurate, than the non-evaluative statement 'The children are sitting on the cat'? We can recognise the difference between an evaluative and a non-evaluative statement, but this does not imply that evaluative statements must be non-factual.

In such examples, where the evaluative content of a statement takes the form of an adjective describing people's characteristics, it is easy to see that an evaluation can also be factual, and thus that it is possible for it to be true or false. Could we say the same about statements such as 'Lying is wrong' or 'You should not drive your car when you are drunk'? Is it possible for such statements to be true? Think about the way in which you would try to show others that such statements were true.

No doubt you would look for some underlying reasons. In order to justify the claim that lying is wrong, you would probably refer to the possible harmful effects on others of being misled. In support of the claim about drunken driving, you would mention the damage to others which drunken drivers can cause. In doing so, you would be offering factual statements in support of evaluative conclusions, and this brings us to the second problem which, it is claimed, afflicts moral arguments – the is/ought gap.

The is/ought gap and support for conclusions

In the last section we pointed out that evaluative statements can be factual. However, there are many factual statements which are not evaluative, but which simply tell us what *is* the case, and make no comment about whether this is good or bad, or whether this ought or ought not to be as it is.

Moral arguments must have evaluative conclusions, but their reasons may be evaluative statements or non-evaluative statements, or a mixture of the two. It is those arguments which move from non-evaluative reasons to evaluative conclusions which give rise to worries about the is/ought gap. These worries are expressed in the following famous passage from the writings of the Scottish philosopher, David Hume (1711–76).

> In every system of morality, which I have hitherto met with, I have always remarked, that the author proceeds for some time in the ordinary way of reasoning, and establishes the being of a God, or makes observations concerning human affairs; when of a sudden I am surprised to find, that instead of the usual copulations of propositions, *is*, and *is not*, I meet with no proposition that is not connected with an ought, or an ought *not*. This change is imperceptible; but is, however, of the last consequence. For as this *ought* or *ought not* expresses some new relation or affirmation, 'tis necessary that it should be observed and explained; and at the same time that a reason should be given, for what seems altogether inconceivable, how this new relation can be a deduction from others, which are entirely different from it.
>
> (Hume, D. (1966) *A Treatise of Human Nature*, Book III, *Of Morals*, London: Dent; New York, Dutton; Everyman's Library, pp. 177-8)

Hume is drawing our attention to the fact that many moral arguments start out by talking about what is the case, and end up talking about what ought to be the case, and he is suggesting that it is difficult to understand how statements about what we ought or ought not to do can follow from statements about what *is* or what *is not*. Based on this observation, many philosophers have been prepared to accept the slogan 'No *ought* from an *is*', that is to say, you cannot derive an evaluative conclusion from non-evaluative reasons.

This view gains reinforcement from another distinction – that between arguments which are deductively valid, and those which are not. It is necessary to explain exactly what is meant by 'deductively valid'. Although in everyday conversation it is quite common to talk about statements being 'valid' – by which we mean that the statement is true – in the field of logic the word 'valid' cannot apply to statements, but only to arguments. When we describe an argument as deductively valid, we are not saying that the reasons and the conclusion are true. We are talking instead about the relationship between the reasons and the conclusion – about the support which the reasons give to the conclusion. An argument is deductively valid if it is not possible for the reasons to be true and yet the conclusion be false. In other words a deductively valid argument is one in which, if the reasons are true, then the conclusion must be true. Here are two examples of deductively valid arguments:

> All insects have only six legs. Spiders have eight legs. So spiders are not insects.

> If he had trained hard, he would have won the race. He didn't win the race. So he can't have trained hard.

In both these arguments, the conclusion follows from the reasons as a matter of logic, such that, provided the reasons are true, the conclusion must be true. In the first argument, the reasons are true, and it is easy to see that the conclusion must be true. You may have thought that the second argument did not provide strong support for the conclusion, because you can imagine someone losing a race even if they trained hard. But this is to question the truth of the first reason, rather than to question the support which the reasons give to the conclusion. This is a deductively valid argument, even though its reasons and conclusion may not be true. If it were true that he would have won the race if he'd trained hard, and that he didn't win the race, then it must be true that he did not train hard.

These two examples are deductively valid because of their structure, which logicians call their 'logical form'. Each of the two arguments above has a structure which it shares with arguments about completely different subjects. It is this structure, and not the subject matter of the argument, which makes the argument deductively valid. We can see the structure if we replace some of the repeated words or phrases in the argument with single letters, as follows:

> If *he had trained hard, he would have won the race*. He didn't win the race. So he can't have trained hard.

Let he trained hard be represented by p, and he won the race be represented by q. The structure of the argument can be set out as:

If p were true, then q would have happened.

q did not happen.

So p cannot be true.

You could try for yourself to work out the structure of the argument about
spiders. In both cases, it is the structure or form of the argument which
makes it deductively valid. There are a number of deductively valid forms of
argument, but we do not need to illustrate all of them.

Some deductively valid arguments are valid not strictly because of their
structure, but because of the meanings of the words they use in the reasons
and the conclusion, for example:

John is Mary's brother.
So Mary is John's sister.

It is true by definition that a female is the sister of her brother.

It is clear that deductively valid arguments provide cast-iron support for
their conclusions, and that any deductively valid argument which has true
reasons is sound in that it indisputably establishes the truth of its conclusion.
Some moral arguments are deductively valid. The first argument we looked at
in this chapter, about lying and withholding information, is both a moral
argument and deductively valid. It is a moral argument because it has an
evaluative conclusion – that withholding information is wrong. It is deductively valid because it would not be possible for its reasons to be true and
yet its conclusion be false (although, as we noted, its reasons may not be
true). But notice that this argument has one evaluative reason – that lying is
wrong. This is what makes it possible for the argument to have a deductively
valid form, as follows:

a is just the same as b.

b is c

So a is c.

By contrast, moral arguments which attempt to establish evaluative
conclusions from non-evaluative reasons will not have a deductively valid

form, and in such arguments it would always be logically possible for the reasons to be true, and the conclusion to be false. Here are two examples which illustrate this point:

> Passive smoking causes cancer. Therefore smoking in public places should be banned.

> Slaughtering animals for food causes pain to animals. So slaughtering animals for food is wrong.

Do these two examples exhibit a deductively valid form? The first one could be expressed as :

> a causes b. Therefore c (which can result in a) should be d.

and the second as:

> a causes b. So a is c.

These two forms are not deductively valid, a point which is probably easier to see if we substitute some new subject matter into these forms, as follows:

> Road accidents cause deaths. Therefore driving dangerously should be encouraged.

> Slimming causes weight loss. So slimming is foolish.

Nor are the examples about passive smoking and about slaughtering animals similar to the Mary and John example, which is deductively valid on the basis of the meanings of the words used in it. 'Causes pain to animals' and 'wrong' are not related *by definition*, in the way in which 'brother' and 'sister' are.

These examples illustrate that many, and possibly all, arguments which move from non-evaluative reasons to an evaluative conclusion do not have a structure in which it would be impossible for the reasons to be true and yet the conclusion be false. Although it is not possible to back up this claim by showing all possible instances of ethical arguments, it should be clear from the above examples that the evaluative term which appears in the conclusion will not be related in a strictly logical way to the non-evaluative phrases which appear in the reasons.

What exactly is the essence of the is/ought problem? Is it that you cannot derive an 'is' from an 'ought' because arguments which start from 'is' statements and draw conclusions about what ought to happen or what we ought to do cannot be deductively valid? If this is what the supposed problem amounts to, then it is a real problem only if it is impossible to have good arguments which are not deductively valid. However, many arguments (including some of those we encountered in Chapter 1) cannot be squeezed into rigid deductively valid forms, and yet they seem to be reasonably good arguments, in the sense that they provide good reasons for accepting the conclusion. Here is an example of such an argument:

> Smith, Jones and Brown all face exactly the same charge, but only Brown has previously been convicted of an offence. It is normal practice for a more severe sentence to be given to someone who has a previous conviction. So if they are all found guilty, Smith and Jones will get lighter sentences than Brown's.

This argument is not deductively valid, because it is possible for the reasons to be true and the conclusion false. It is possible that although it is normal practice to give more severe sentences to those with previous convictions, and only Brown has a previous conviction, Smith and Jones will not get lighter sentences than Brown's. Perhaps all three will get equally harsh sentences, if, for example, the judge wants to set an example to others. Yet this argument presents quite good reasons for thinking that Smith and Jones will get lighter sentences than Brown's. It is not a bad argument, even though it is not deductively valid. Can some moral arguments be good arguments, even though they are not deductively valid?

Perhaps those who insist that there is a problem about the move from 'is' to 'ought' are making a stronger claim than that moral arguments with non-evaluative reasons cannot be deductively valid. They may accept that some non-moral arguments which fail the test for deductive validity can be good arguments, but insist that 'is' statements can never be good reasons for accepting conclusions about what one ought to do or about what is morally right or morally wrong. Most of us do not live our lives as moral sceptics of this kind. We do take non-evaluative statements as good reasons for evaluative conclusions. If a child asks 'Why shouldn't I hit my sister?', you will think you have given a good reason if you reply 'Because it hurts her'. There may be some people who do not take such reasons as moral considerations, and with such people we probably cannot engage in moral reasoning. This does not show that moral reasoning is not possible or that moral arguments cannot be assessed. It merely shows that such reasoning rests upon some basic moral responses which are taken for granted. Indeed, in moral disputes there is often agreement about some basic moral principle, but disagreement about facts or about whether the principle applies to the case under discussion. Remember our earlier argument:

> Passive smoking causes cancer. Therefore smoking in public places should be banned.

Those who disagree with the conclusion of this argument are not likely to say that causing harm to others is not a moral consideration. They are more likely to dispute the evidence that passive smoking causes cancer; or to disagree with the assumption that if people smoke in public places, passive smoking is inevitable; or to claim that the restriction of smokers' liberty is a greater harm than putting others at risk from passive smoking.

Our examination of the two supposed problems for moral arguments – the fact/value distinction and the is/ought gap – has shown that they are not obstacles to the assessment of moral reasoning. It is the mark of the reasonable person, not the unreasonable, to take some facts as good reasons for moral conclusions; and those who are reluctant to talk of the *truth* of evaluative statements will no doubt be willing to concede that certain basic moral evaluations are *acceptable*.

Truth of reasons and reliability of authorities

Amongst the reasons presented for moral conclusions there will be some non-evaluative statements. Let us consider how we might assess the truth of such reasons. It is obvious that no-one will be in a position to know whether all the reasons presented in all the arguments they may encounter are true. However, we all have a share in a body of common knowledge, many of us have detailed knowledge about our particular field of work or study, and we have some ideas about whom to trust to give us correct information on subjects which are less familiar to us.

Common knowledge can take us a long way in assessing many of the short arguments we looked at earlier. For example, in the following argument which appeared in Chapter 1, the reasons are items of common knowledge, and assessment of their truth requires no special expertise.

> Being aware of the dangers of driving too fast is not sufficient to stop people from speeding. Many drivers are still exceeding speed limits. A recent television campaign has emphasised the dangers of driving too fast, by showing home videos of children who were subsequently killed by speeding motorists.

The first reason claims that many drivers are still exceeding speed limits. It is easy to find out if this true, simply by being in a car which is travelling within the speed limits, and observing whether many drivers overtake. The second reason is that there has been a television campaign emphasising the dangers of speeding. Most people will know that this is true, because they will have seen the publicity for themselves. Those who have not actually seen it will be able to ask others about it. Of course, this means that they are relying on others in order to assess the truth of reasons, and this is something which we often have to do. Not all the information we get about the world comes to us first-hand, nor could it. We simply have to accept that no-one has time to become an expert on everything, but this doesn't mean that the only information about which we can be confident is the information which we get for ourselves. There are sensible ways of assessing whether the information which others give us is reliable, and for the most part these involve an awareness of characteristics or circumstances which make evidence unreliable.

The most obvious case of unreliability concerns people with a record of misleading others or of being untruthful. Sometimes people who are in general truthful want to mislead others because they have something to gain by doing so or something to lose by telling the truth. However, even people who are not trying to deceive us can give us inaccurate information, so we need to think about the circumstances in which people might make mistakes.

We need to know whether our informant is in a position to have the supposed knowledge. If specialised knowledge is involved, is the person an expert in the relevant field? If eye-witness testimony is crucial, was the person in a position to see clearly what was happening? Are there any factors which might influence the person's judgement? Our judgements may be less reliable if we are under the influence of alcohol or drugs, or if we are suffering from stress, or if we are distracted by other events.

Often we can get information about the same topic from a number of different sources. When we get the same information from a number of sources, then, provided we have no reason to judge them unreliable in accordance with the criteria mentioned above, we can have more confidence in the accuracy of the information.

The factors to take into account when assessing the reliability of evidence or authorities are summarised below.

Summary

1 *Is this person likely to be telling a lie, to be failing to give full relevant information, or to be attempting to mislead?*

(a) Do they have a record of being untruthful?

(b) Do they have a reason for being untruthful?

e.g. would they gain something very important by deceiving me?
would they lose something very important by telling the truth?

2 *Is this person in a position to have the relevant knowledge?*

(a) If expert knowledge is involved, are they expert, or have they been informed by an expert?

(b) If first-hand experience is important, were they in a position to have that experience?

e.g. if observation is involved, could they see and hear clearly?

3 *Are there any factors which would interfere with the accuracy of this person's judgement?*

(a) Was, or is, the person under emotional stress?

(b) Was, or is, the person under the influence of alcohol or drugs?

(c) Was the person likely to have been distracted by other events?

(d) Does the person have a strong desire or incentive to believe one version of events, or one explanation, rather than another?

(e) In the case of first-hand experience of an event, was information obtained from the person immediately following the event?

4 *Is there evidence from another source which corroborates this person's statement?*

Assessing support for conclusions

Reasons can support conclusions in different ways. For example, arguments may use past experience as evidence for their conclusions, or may draw their conclusions on the basis of what is true of similar cases. They may present scientific evidence, or offer general principles which have implications for particular cases.

In addition to differences in the *type* of support which reasons give to conclusions, there can be variations in the *strength* of support. We have already observed that deductively valid arguments give the strongest possible support to their conclusions, and also that arguments which give less strong support to their conclusions can nevertheless be good arguments.

When assessing the strength of support within an argument, it is useful to ask ourselves the following questions:

1 Are the reasons/evidence relevant to the conclusion?

2 If so, do the reasons/evidence provide a good basis for accepting the conclusion?

3 If the conclusion recommends some action or policy, would it be reasonable to act on the basis of the reasons/evidence?

4 Can I think of any other evidence, not mentioned in the argument, which would weaken or strengthen the conclusion?

5 Can I draw any conclusions from the information in the passage, and do these conclusions support or undermine the author's conclusion?

We can put this into practice with two examples.

> Adopted children should be told early in their life that they have been adopted. The first reason for this concerns the importance to the child of a sense of identity. The second reason is the wider one of children and truth in general. If parents are found once to have lied they will not again be believed. You must always work on the basis that children will eventually find out, and when they do, they will have to deal not only with the fact of discovery but also the fact that they have been deceived by the people they trusted most.
>
> (Adapted from Carol Sarler, 'When to Tell a Child Who Her Father Is',
> *Independent on Sunday*, 23 June 1996)

Remember that for the moment we are simply considering whether the reasons, *if true*, give support to the conclusion, so we do not need to ask whether the reasons are true. Let's assume they are. One reason offered for the conclusion that adopted children should be told at an early age about their adoption is that a sense of identity is important to the child. Is this relevant to the conclusion? It is somewhat difficult to assess its relevance because not enough is said about the connection between children's sense of identity and knowledge of their origins. Perhaps adopted children can develop a strong sense of identity from their relationship with their adoptive parents. So without further explanation as to why this point is relevant, this does not seem to be a very strong reason for the conclusion. The second theme in the reasoning is that since adopted children will at some stage find out that they are adopted, they will cease to trust their adoptive parents, and they will have to cope, not with one, but with two potentially distressing discoveries – that they have been adopted, and that they have been deceived. If these claims are true, they seem to provide good reason to act on the recommendation which the argument makes. If it is true that children will find out anyway, and that this will cause more distress than being told by their adoptive parents, then it would be sensible for parents concerned about their children's welfare to tell them at an early stage that they are adopted. If it is true also that children who find out they have been deceived cease to trust their parents, then any adoptive parents who wish to retain their children's trust would be wise to give them the information. As for further evidence, if it were found that those who cease to trust their parents also find it more difficult to trust others in their adult life, this would add additional weight to the argument. Conversely, if it were found that very young children suffer great distress on being told they are adopted, this would count against the conclusion.

For our second example, let us look again at this argument which first appeared in Chapter 1:

> The Italians, who drink a lot of wine and eat a diet rich in fruit, vegetables and olive oil, have a lower incidence of heart disease than the British. The British government should therefore encourage its citizens to increase their consumption of wine, fruit, vegetables and olive oil, so that its citizens will be less susceptible to heart attacks.

When we first looked at this argument, we noticed that it was not clear whether the conclusion was claiming that the British government has a moral obligation towards its citizens, or simply that if the government wants its citizens to be less susceptible to heart attacks, it should follow the recommendation given in the conclusion. As the argument stands, it gives no explicit reason for accepting that the government has moral obligations concerning the health of its citizens. Such a conclusion would have to rely on an unstated assumption that governments in general have obligations concerning the health of their citizens. Perhaps this is not an unreasonable assumption, in that it does seem to be the proper responsibility of governments to ensure that their people are protected by legislation about, for example, safe water supplies and pollution which threatens life or health. But it is questionable how far governments should go to encourage people to change their diet. It is reasonable to accept that the government has a duty to publicise information about health risks from certain foods, but if 'encouragement' went to the lengths of preaching to the public or subsidising certain healthy foods and taxing unhealthy ones, this may be regarded as an unacceptable infringement of freedom of choice.

Both possible interpretations of the conclusion rest upon the claims in the first sentence that the Italians consume a great deal of wine, fruit, vegetables and olive oil, and do not suffer much heart disease. Since what we are focusing on in this section is support for conclusions, let us assume that these claims are true, and ask, do they show that if the British changed to an Italian diet, they would be less susceptible to heart disease? First, are the details about the Italian diet relevant to the conclusion? Well, it is evidence which is worth taking into account when we are wondering how the incidence of heart disease amongst the British might be reduced. It certainly isn't irrelevant, provided we can make the widely accepted assumption that diet can have an effect on health. But is it sufficient to give strong support to the conclusion? The problem is that we cannot be sure from this one example what relationship there is between the kind of diet which Italians have, and their low incidence of heart disease. Perhaps they are genetically less susceptible to heart disease than are the British, and maybe their diet makes no difference. Or perhaps the crucial difference is something which is *excluded* from the Italian diet, and *included* in the British diet, in which case all the wine, olive oil, fruit and vegetables in the world may not save us. This is a case in which it is important to look for further evidence – perhaps of diets and heart disease rates in a range of countries, or differences in diet and heart disease rates within the British population. In the *Independent* newspaper on 27 September 1996, the following report of a study of diet and health appeared:

> Scientists recorded the eating habits and health of almost 11,000 people over 17 years, and found that there were 32 per cent fewer deaths from strokes and 24 per cent fewer deaths from heart attacks in people who ate fresh fruit every day.

This suggests that the significant difference between the typical Italian diet and the British diet may be the consumption of fresh fruit, so perhaps the argument recommends a greater change in diet than is necessary. There is insufficient evidence in the argument to give strong support to the conclusion.

Flaws in arguments

When the reasons offered in an argument give no support at all to the conclusion, we can describe the argument as having a flaw. There are a number of ways in which reasoning can be flawed, and we mention some of the most common flaws below.

Correlation/causation

Sometimes people assume that because two things regularly occur together, one of them must cause the other. The regular association between two different things is called a correlation. A correlation has been established if whenever we find *x*, we are likely to find *y*, or whenever a person or a population has characteristic *x*, they are likely to have characteristic *y*. But the discovery of such an association cannot, by itself, tell us that *x* causes *y*. For example, suppose you discover that children who frequently watch violent videos are likely to be aggressive; this may be because watching violent videos causes aggressive behaviour, or it may be because a natural tendency to aggressive behaviour causes children to enjoy watching violent videos. Or suppose you find that people who have a great deal of tooth decay tend to be overweight. This may be because a third factor – perhaps eating large amounts of sugary foods – causes both these conditions. Some correlations may simply be coincidences, with no causal connections at all between the two factors. This was why the argument about the Italian diet and heart disease was not a very strong one. However, that argument was not completely off track, because although it didn't mention connections between diet and disease, it is generally accepted that such connections exist.

Necessary/sufficient conditions

Another common flaw in reasoning is to treat a necessary condition as if it were a sufficient condition. For example, someone may argue that because hard work is necessary in order to get a good grade on a course, anyone who works hard will get a good grade. But this conclusion does not follow, because there may be other conditions which are necessary in order to get a good grade – for example, a certain level of intelligence – and hard work alone, though necessary, may not be sufficient.

Unwarranted generalisation

Another common flaw is to draw a general conclusion on the basis of just one known case. For example, if we drew the conclusion that social workers are busybodies from our knowledge of one social worker who had this characteristic, we would be guilty of flawed reasoning.

These are some of the most common flaws, but you are likely to find others when you are assessing reasoning. What you need to develop is the ability to say exactly why a conclusion does not follow from the reasons which are offered for it. A more detailed list of fallacies in reasoning can be found in Nigel Warburton's book *Thinking from A to Z*, and exercises in identifying flaws appear in Anne Thomson's *Critical Reasoning – A Practical Introduction*.

Some arguments which use analogies can be flawed, and since the use of analogy can occur in moral arguments, it is useful to look specifically at an example of assessment of analogy.

Assessing analogies and comparisons

In Chapter 1 we discussed briefly the use of both explicit and implicit comparisons in reasoning. With explicit comparisons, such as 'Withholding information is just the same as lying', it will be obvious which two things are being compared. With implicit comparisons, we shall have to identify the two things which are assumed to be analogous before we attempt to assess the analogy. Analogies do not always rely on factual examples; writers may set up an imaginary scenario in order to elicit a particular response from their readers. This happens in the following example.

> Although I have no facts or figures, still I find it reasonable to suppose that the average citizen of the typical underdeveloped country works as hard as the average American. Quite possibly he works harder. At any rate it seems a little unlikely that the average American (or perhaps I had better say the average reader of this book) actually believes he is more important or worthy or whatever than the average Asian, African, or Latin American, and still more unlikely that he could be correct in so believing. Surely the typical American, at least if he would stop to think about it, would admit that he was no better a person and no harder a worker than the average Asian, and that their extreme difference in station sprung wholly and simply from the accident of the one's being born in America and the other's in Asia. So why should one get all the money while the other starves?
>
> Imagine a factory-owner who hires 45 people to work for him. All the employees work equally hard, but when time comes to pay them, the owner entrusts all their salaries to one of them and (for some strange reason) leaves it totally up to this one worker how much each of the others shall be paid. What would you think of that worker if he kept all or so nearly all the money for himself that the other 44 were always in dire poverty and ten of them eventually died of starvation? Is he not guilty (morally if not legally) of stealing the others' money; and if he knew some would die because of his theft, is he not also guilty of murder? And is not this the situation of the average American – by an odd quirk of fate entrusted with the salaries of 45 human beings and empowered to dispense the money at his whim? And keeping all of it for himself, leaving them to starve? Killing them in order to steal their money? If he does not want to be guilty of these charges, then let him give back their money, or else explain how by keeping it nearly all for himself, he has distributed it fairly –why he deserves to bask while they grovel.
>
> (Louis Pascal, 'Judgement Day' in P. Singer (ed.) 1986a: pp.112–13)

The most striking comparison here is between an imaginary worker and the average American. The worker, though making no more effort than his fellow workers, has been given the money for all the workers' salaries, and left to distribute it as he wishes. We are invited to see this worker as analogous to the average American, who works no harder than the inhabitants of poorer countries, yet, by a stroke of good fortune, has been granted wealth whilst others have nothing. If we think that it would be wrong for the worker to keep all or most of the money whilst others starved, then, so the argument suggests, it is wrong for average Americans to keep their money whilst people in some countries are in poverty.

How are we to assess this analogy? We need to know whether the two things which are being compared really are alike in all the important respects, or are there differences between them which make a difference to the conclusion which is drawn. In what ways, then, is the average American like the imaginary worker? Both are enjoying relative wealth while others who work as hard as they do, and who, we assume, are no less worthy than they, are poor or starving. There are differences. The money given to the imaginary worker represents some appropriate remuneration for the total amount of work done, and the worker knows he has not done all of it, so how can he possibly think he is entitled to all of it? Moreover, giving others their fair share would be a very simple matter, requiring no intermediaries, and leaving him certain that the money had reached the person entitled to it. The responsibility for the distribution of the money is his and his alone. By contrast, average Americans have some reason to believe they are entitled to their income since they have received what is deemed to be the appropriate remuneration for their labour in the country in which they live; even if they wished to bring about some global redistribution of income, it would be difficult for them to be certain that their donations actually reached those in poverty; and the responsibility for such redistribution does not rest with any single individual American. Nevertheless this is a striking analogy, and one which should prompt us to think that even if each individual American does not have a responsibility to give away their wealth to the starving, at least wealthy nations should attempt to share their wealth with poorer nations.

This passage contains two other interesting comparisons. The first is between the average Asian, African and Latin American on the one hand, and the average American on the other. They are claimed to work equally hard and to be equal in importance and worthiness, and from this we are intended to conclude that one group should not starve while the other gets all the money.

The other implicit comparison in the second paragraph is between certain actions and certain failures to act – for example, between stealing and not sharing out money, between murder and not preventing someone from starving to death. In each case it is implied that the act and the omission are equivalent because they bring about the same result, and hence that someone who is guilty of omission is just as bad as someone who commits the evil act. Think about whether acts and omissions in these examples are exactly the same. What differences are there between them which might suggest that failure to act is not as morally bad as an action, when the failure and the action have exactly the same result? We shall return to this topic in Chapter 6.

In summary, the important questions to ask about analogies are:

What exactly are the two things which are being compared?
Are there any relevant differences between them?

Summarising the skills of assessment

Here is a checklist to work through when assessing the reasoning in the passages in Exercise 3.

1 Find the conclusion.
2 Find the reasons and any unstated assumptions.
3 Consider how far you can go in assessing the truth of the reasons and the unstated assumptions. Think about how you would seek further information to enable you to assess the truth of reasons.
4 Does the reasoning rely on evidence from sources whose authority is questionable?
5 Do you yourself have any knowledge which strengthens or weakens the conclusion? (Remember to subject your own 'knowledge' to the same standards of scrutiny as you apply to the claims made by other people!)
6 Can you draw any conclusions which have not been mentioned by the author?
7 Does the passage contain any explanations? If so, are they plausible, and are they the only plausible explanations of what is being explained?
8 Does the argument rely on any analogies or comparisons. If so, are the two things which are being compared alike in all relevant respects?
9 Assess the strength of the support which the reasons give to the conclusion. If you believe that the conclusion is not well supported by the reasons and assumptions, can you state the way in which the move from reasons to conclusion is flawed?

Exercise 3 Assessing moral reasoning

Identify and assess the reasoning in each of the following passages.

Make a note of any moral concepts which are used. You will find comments in Appendix 1 on those items marked with an asterisk.

1* There should be a law against parents hitting their children. Children are much more likely to be well behaved if parents use other kinds of punishment than physical violence.

2 Although we could reduce road accidents by lowering speed limits, and making greater efforts to ensure that such limits are enforced, this would inconvenience the majority who drive safely. Therefore, it would be an unacceptable solution to the problem of careless drivers who are unsafe at current speed limits.

3* We are right to assume that children should not be exposed to publicity. Children might not agree; most are dazzled by the idea of any kind of fame. But then, many children probably want to drink, smoke, gamble or have sex. Publicity is like all of those things: habit-forming and life-changing. They all require a reasonably mature mind to grasp their implications. Making a child famous, as Michael Jackson should testify, is risky.

(Adapted from Bryan Appleyard, 'Glare That Marks For Life', *Independent*, 30 January 1996)

4 If you cannot be absolutely certain that every person owning a handgun will be safe, then there is only one possible course of action: the banning of the private use of handguns. Handguns are only used for a pastime – target shooting – but were designed for another purpose, killing, and are the most dangerous of weapons. They are easily concealed. Handgun owners claim they have a 'right' to shoot and that the vast majority of them are responsible. However, if we are to compare rights, the 'right' to own a gun comes very low down on a scale in which the right to be safe and protected from lethal weapons and the right to life are paramount.

(Adapted from Michael North, 'Licence to Kill Must be Revoked', *The Times Higher Education Supplement*, 27 September 1996)

5* We in the rich nations are like the occupants of a crowded lifeboat adrift in a sea full of drowning people. If we try to save the drowning by bringing them aboard, our boat will be overloaded and we shall all drown. Since it is better that some survive than none, we should leave the others to drown. In the world today...'lifeboat ethics' apply. The rich should leave the poor to starve, for otherwise the poor will drag the rich down with them.
(Peter Singer's version of an argument by Garrett Hardin, Singer, *Practical Ethics*, 1993 p. 236)

6 Life in prison is still life, however unpleasant. In contrast, the death penalty does not just threaten to make life unpleasant – it threatens to take life altogether. This difference is perceived by those affected. We find that when they have the choice between life in prison and execution, 99 per cent of all prisoners under sentence of death prefer life in prison...

From this unquestioned fact a reasonable conclusion can be drawn in favour of the superior deterrent effect of the death penalty. Those who have the choice in practice...fear death more than they fear life in prison...If they do, it follows that the threat of the death penalty, all other things equal, is likely to deter more than the threat of life in prison. One is most deterred by what one fears most. From which it follows that whatever statistics fail, or do not fail, to show, the death penalty is likely to be more deterrent than any other.
(E. Van den Haag (1983) *The Death Penalty: A Debate*, New York: Plenum, pp. 68–69)

7* When asked the commonplace question, 'Why bother about endangered species', there are a host of possible answers: because other creatures have a basic right in themselves to be treated as equally valuable expressions of evolution as we humans; because our own self-interest may depend on some future use we come to make of these species or the habitats on which they depend; because we have no right to deprive future generations of their enjoyment or use of these creatures. But more important than all of these is the fact that we owe it to ourselves, right here and now, to fulfil our obligation to act as stewards of the heaving and mysterious multitude of life.
(Jonathon Porritt, *Independent*, 15 October 1996)

8 If a parent was so depressed that she wanted to kill herself and her children, we wouldn't respond by helping her to do this in the most efficient way. Instead, she would be offered treatment or counselling aimed at changing her desire. Why, then, should we treat the desire to kill an unborn child in a different way? For women who want abortions, our laws allow for medical help to get rid of the unborn child by the method which will be least dangerous to the pregnant woman. What we should do instead is to change the desires of such women by offering emotional support to enable them to go through with a pregnancy. So long as abortion is legal, the incidence of it will not decrease. Making it illegal would not eliminate it, but it would be likely to reduce the numbers seeking abortions, and that, after all, is what we should be aiming for.

9* The US constitution forbids religious worship or teaching in state schools. Now is the time for us to follow suit. For once some are allowed sectarian education, there is no reason why others shouldn't be allowed their schools too – New Agers, astrologists, Moonies or any other sect or cult with a sufficient number of followers. After all, if you really believe the stars govern our everyday lives, then of course children should be taught the details of the movements and influences of the planets and the zodiac. If you think that's all nonsense but the Bible is the literal truth, be warned, for there is no satisfactory legal definition of a religion. A religion is just a cult with more followers.

(Polly Toynbee, *Independent*, 23 October 1997)

10 No matter how much the hunting lobby bray about the thrill of the chase and the skill of the riders, one simple fact remains: the end purpose of this sport is death. Killing for food, killing for protection, killing to manage the countryside; all these are essential and we shouldn't be squeamish about them. But the idea that people could be so proud of enjoying the kill is rather repellent.

Tradition is no defence. The fact that families have been playing such games for centuries doesn't justify their heirs continuing to hunt today. For centuries people have been doing all sorts of appalling things – including badger baiting, cockfighting and working ponies until they dropped – that we have now made illegal. Compassion about animals isn't a fad for flaky urbanites, nor is it simply squeamishness; it is a measure of a society becoming gentler and more civilised. This newspaper wouldn't hunt.

But would we, therefore, ban it? We would not: the prospect of the state intervening to ban an activity where the harm to others is not overwhelming troubles us deeply.

('Beware of the Anti-Hunting Roundheads in Full Cry', leading article in the *Independent*, 24 December 1996)

Assessing principles

In Chapter 1 we mentioned two features which are frequently found in ethical arguments – moral concepts and moral principles. We shall have to be able to assess their use in order to make a thorough assessment of moral reasoning. In the case of principles, this involves drawing out the implications, thinking about what follows from a particular principle.

This activity is closely related to the skills which you have already practised. In assessing other people's arguments, you have been thinking about what does and what does not follow from the reasons presented. Hence, although you have not explicitly been offered exercises in drawing your own conclusions, you will inevitably have been doing this.

Working out the implications of principles is just another aspect of drawing conclusions. It involves thinking about all the cases to which the principle must apply. People often justify their ethical position on a particular topic by relying, explicitly or implicitly, on a general principle. If we can identify other cases to which the principle applies, we may be able to assess whether there is something wrong with the principle, and thus whether it should be rejected or modified.

We have already seen some examples of principles. 'Lying is wrong' is a principle, which, if we are to accept it, must apply to all cases of knowingly making a false statement with the intention of deceiving others. It implies that just as it is wrong to lie about your income on your tax return, and to lie to your partner about having an affair, it is wrong to tell your friend that a hat suits her when it doesn't, and to tell the Nazis that you do not know where a Jewish family is hiding, even though you do know. Some of these applications may suggest to us that the principle is too sweeping, and that it should be modified to allow for certain important exceptions.

This is the simple strategy to follow when assessing a principle: think about as many cases as possible to which it must apply; consider whether any of these applications shows that there is something wrong with the principle; think about the way in which the principle should be modified. You could try this for yourself with principles such as 'Killing is wrong' and 'Dangerous sports should be banned'.

Sometimes, rather than concluding that we should modify a principle, we may conclude that we should reject it completely, either because all of its applications are ethically suspect, or because it is difficult to judge which instances actually fall under the principle. Let us illustrate this with the following example, which concerns decisions about priorities in the National Health Service. The following paragraph appeared in the *Guardian* on 29 April 1992 in the context of a discussion about how the Health Service should decide which patients to treat when financial resources cannot meet the demand for treatment.

> Alan Williams, professor of economics at York University, reports in the latest issue of the Journal of Medical Ethics that when he asked 80 people how the National Health Service should discriminate among patients, the biggest single group of those stating a preference said priority should go to those who had cared for their health at the expense of those who had not.
>
> (David Brindle, 'Whose Lifeline is it Anyway?', *Guardian*, 29 April 1992)

If we assume that the people questioned by Alan Williams constituted a representative sample of the British population, this suggests that there would be some support among the population for the principle 'Medical treatment for those who have not cared for their health should be given a lower priority than treatment for those who have taken care of their health'.

The first problem for assessing this principle is working out who comes into the category of 'people who have not cared for their health'. Does it include everyone who has engaged in activities which cause illness, such as smoking, excessive consumption of alcohol, having an unhealthy diet? Perhaps not, because some of the people who have an unhealthy diet may not be aware that their diet could lead to illness. How can we say that they are not taking care of their health when they don't know that their lifestyle is bad for their health? There is a very real practical difficulty here, because it would be almost impossible to distinguish between those who know that their diet is bad for health, but are willing to take the risk, and those who do not realise that their diet puts their health at risk.

The same problem occurs when we consider smokers. There may be some smokers who want to give up smoking because they know it is bad for their health, but find that they cannot do so, however hard they try. Are they to be put into the same category as smokers who don't care about the health risks?

Suppose we could make the right judgements about such cases, and thus give lower priority only to those who knew that their lifestyle was bad for their health, and who had the capacity to change their habits (as people who are addicted to, for example, drugs, alcohol and nicotine may not). Even then, the further implications of this principle may tell us that the principle is unacceptable, not just because it is impractical, but because it has unethical implications. It would mean, for example, that motor cyclists with head injuries should not be given priority for treatment if they were not wearing a crash helmet, and that rock climbers should not be given priority for treatment of injuries due to climbing accidents.

This discussion of the assessment of principles has highlighted another important aspect of assessing reasoning – the need to be clear about what exactly is meant by terms and phrases used in arguments.

Clarifying terms

In the previous section we sought to clarify the meaning of the phrase 'people who have not taken care of their health'. You may find when reading passages of reasoning that there are some ambiguous words and phrases, and that you cannot thoroughly assess the reasoning until you have sorted out what exactly is meant by the word or phrase. Authors may deliberately use ambiguous language in order to get their readers to accept a conclusion which is not well supported. More often, authors may not notice an ambiguity, so we should not assume that all cases of lack of clarity are attempts to mislead.

One of the most important aspects of clarification in relation to ethical reasoning is to have a clear understanding of the implications of any moral concepts which are used. We shall devote Chapter 5 to the clarification of ethical concepts. Meanwhile, as you work through the exercises in Chapter 3, try to clarify to your own satisfaction any unclear terms and phrases which you find. Make a note of ethical concepts which are used. When you do the decision making exercises in Chapter 4, try to be consistent in the way in which you use ethical concepts.

Exercising the skills of reasoning

The exercises which you have done so far have presented you with short passages of reasoning, and have not always asked you to use the whole range of skills involved in analysis and assessment of reasoning. Now is the time to put together all these skills, and to use them on longer passages of reasoning, more typical of discussions which you will find on practical ethical issues in newspapers, journals and textbooks.

With these longer passages, you may have to sift relevant from irrelevant material, and sort out a jumble of reasons and conclusions, rather than finding a linear progression from basic reasons via intermediate conclusions to a main conclusion. It can be helpful to write a brief summary of a long passage, before getting down to sorting out exactly how its reasoning fits together. Your summary should take the following form:

> This passage is trying to convince me that.[main conclusion].,. on the grounds that first, .[major reason].,. second.[another major reason], and so on.

Once you have an outline like this, it should not be too difficult to fill in the more detailed parts of the reasoning, such as the basic reasons and any unstated assumptions which may support the major reasons.

When the structure of the reasoning has been sorted out, you simply take the same steps as you took for Exercise 3, with an additional step which identifies and assesses any principles found in the passage. Here is another summary of these steps.

Summary

1 Find the conclusion.
2 Find the reasons and any unstated assumptions.
3 Consider how far you can go in assessing the truth of the reasons and the unstated assumptions. Think about how you would seek further information to enable you to assess the truth of reasons.
4 Does the reasoning rely on evidence from sources whose authority is questionable?
5 Do you yourself have any knowledge which strengthens or weakens the conclusion?
6 Can you draw any conclusions which have not been mentioned by the author?
7 Does the passage contain any explanations? If so, are they plausible, and are they the only plausible explanations of what is being explained?
8 Does the argument rely on any analogies or comparisons. If so, are the two things which are being compared alike in all relevant respects?
9 Identify and assess any principles upon which the passage relies.
10 Assess the strength of the support which the reasons give to the conclusion. If you believe that the conclusion is not well supported by the reasons and assumptions, can you state the way in which the move from reasons to conclusion is flawed?

With the following two examples, we illustrate how the method can be used. The analysis and assessment offered for each example is very detailed. You may find it difficult to produce something as detailed as this on your first attempt, but you can aim to work towards this kind of analysis, starting with the passages in Exercise 4.

Example 1: Time to consent to change – Edwina Currie

If politicians have learnt anything recently it is not to moralise about other people's behaviour. No doubt many colleagues, along with the public, deplore the whole idea of homosexuality. That doesn't mean we should ban it. We cannot simply write our personal moral attitudes into a law which applies blindly to everybody. It doesn't work anyway, and that sets the worst example of all for our young people. They soon get the idea that they can ignore great chunks of other law, too.

The argument for changing the law to reduce the age of consent for gay men from the present age of 21 can be put in a more pragmatic way. In a free society, the onus is on those who discriminate to explain its practical benefits. For example, we all want to shield youngsters – boys and girls – from predatory adults. Yet if a boy wished, today, to make a complaint about an unwanted homosexual approach, he would think twice about telling the authorities – for it would be *he* who was questioned, and he might well face charges himself. So the current law acts not to protect, but to enforce silence. Who would seek help in these circumstances?

We faced a dilemma in Department of Health in the mid-1980s when we needed to warn young gay men of the mortal dangers of promiscuity. Talking to them about safe sex, we realised, meant asking health workers to seek out boys who were seriously breaking the law. We decided to go ahead anyway, for safety's sake: if our Aids death figures are now lower than everyone predicted, that wise decision takes the credit. How much easier, and more effective, if criminality was not at issue.

We should be clear that 'consent' means exactly that. If consent is withheld, then sex is illegal. In recent years, to my relief, it has been accepted that when a woman says no, she is entitled to be taken at her word. The same applies to young men too. Then there is the pressure that can come from an older person or one in a position of authority. That happens when young girls are involved as well; homosexuals have no monopoly on unpleasant behaviour. But it's against the law, and will rightly stay that way.

The House of Commons might prefer to reduce the age of consent to 18 rather than 16. This has a neat air of compromise and would reduce the discrimination against many gay men: a substantial net gain. But it would not be just, and it would not stick. The position is illogical. How could anyone accept that a young man of 17 is capable of giving informed consent if he falls for a girl – to the point where he can marry – but not if his inclinations are the other way? By the time I was 16, I knew that I liked boys, and nothing whatever has dissuaded me since. My gay friends say the same. All the medical evidence suggests that sexuality is settled quite young, certainly before 18.

Some people will never accept that for many people homosexuality is a way of life. Isn't it a disease which should be wiped out? Shouldn't we be taking every step to avoid further infection, particularly of the young? That is the assumption underlying all our institutions, including the criminal law, which forbids all homosexual acts under the age of 21, even though both parties – long since old enough to vote, or join the forces, or sleep with a girl – have given informed consent.

I was astonished to discover that the Commons had never seriously debated change since the Sexual Offences Act of 1967 made homosexuality legal in England and Wales. Scotland did not follow until 1980, and it was banned in Ulster until 1982.

Here is an outmoded law which touches, at the most conservative estimate, a million of our fellow citizens who are gay. Such men pay their taxes and hold down jobs; their ranks have included distinguished actors, composers, writers and artists, soldiers and politicians. They run banks and businesses at the highest level. Yet on this one topic, their personal judgement is regarded as dangerous: the State decides who they may and may not love. Surely this is, and always has been, absolute nonsense.

Most countries have equal ages of consent, often lower than ours. In Italy it is 14; in Holland, Greece, France, Poland and Sweden it is 15; in Norway, Belgium, Portugal and Switzerland, 16. The German government has announced that it will introduce equal age legislation, and the Irish government did so successfully last spring, at 17. In none of these sober, intelligent countries did the dire events transpire which have been predicted for Britain.

Parliament is at its best when it faces a clear issue of conscience. The welfare and human rights of a large group of our voters are at stake. I have always sought equality and respect in my own life. I will now vote for equality for others, and hope for a clear result to carry this country forward.

(*The Times*, 13 January 1994)

We shall work through the steps set out earlier. Our initial summary would consist of the details given under point 1 and point 2, (i) to (viii) below.

1 *Conclusion*

The passage is trying to convince us that the age of consent for engaging in homosexual acts should be changed from 21 to 16.

2 *Reasons and assumptions*

The reasons offered for this are:

(i)   We should not have laws which are not going to be respected.

(ii) In a free society any discrimination must be shown to have practical benefits.

(iii) Discrimination against homosexuals with regard to the age of consent has no practical benefits.

(iv) It would be less difficult to advise young homosexuals about safe sex if their actions were not classified as criminal.

(v)   It would be illogical to reduce the age of consent for homosexual acts to 18.

(vi) Homosexuality is not a disease to be stamped out.

(vii) Most countries have equal ages of consent for homosexuals and heterosexuals, often lower than ours – with no problems.

(viii) Changing the law in this way would give equality to, and show respect for, homosexuals.

Support is offered for reason (i) by the claim that if we have a particular law which is not respected, people will tend to think that it is acceptable to ignore other laws also.

Support is offered for reason (iii) by attempting to show that the benefit which the higher age of consent for homosexual acts is supposed to have – protection of the young from unwanted sexual advances – does not exist. The author argues that young men who wished to complain about unwanted sexual advances would be reluctant to do so as long as homosexuality was a criminal offence for people in their age group, because they would fear prosecution themselves. Additional support is offered in the fourth paragraph with the suggestion that if homosexual acts were legal from the age of 16, then young people who did not consent – whether male or female – would be protected by law in any case, because 'if consent is withheld, then sex is illegal'.

Support for reason (iv) takes the form of an example – the Department of Health's attempts in the mid-1980s to warn young gay men about the risk of Aids. The author claims that this exercise would have been easier and more effective if criminality were not at stake.

Reason (v) – concerning the illogicality of reducing the age of consent to 18 rather than 16 – is supported by the observation that it is inconsistent to believe that a young man of 17 is capable of informed consent to heterosexual acts, but incapable of informed consent if he wishes to engage in homosexual acts. There is an additional claim that 'all the medical evidence suggests that sexuality is settled quite young, certainly before 18'. This could be taken to give additional support to reason (iv), showing that not only is it *inconsistent* to think that 17-year-olds are incapable of giving informed consent to homosexual acts, it is also *mistaken*.

To support reason (vi), the author lists respected professions in which homosexuals can be found. This is intended to show that such people are capable of making rational decisions about how to run their lives, and that no-one should be able to judge better than they can whom 'they may and may not love'. It is possible that the comments about sexuality being settled early are also meant to support the claim that homosexuality is not something which people can be 'infected', as they can with a disease.

Reason (vii) is given support with a list of countries with equal ages of consent for homosexuals and heterosexuals.

Some of the reasons listed above (e.g. (iii) and (vi)), are not explicitly stated, so it is appropriate to list these as assumptions.

There is also an assumption that it is appropriate that the age of consent for heterosexual acts should be 16.

There is an assumption that we should act in accordance with the principles of equality and respect.

3 *Truth of reasons and assumptions*

The basic claim which is meant to support reason (i) is questionable. Those who flout a law which they believe to be a bad law will not necessarily cease to respect other laws.

Reason (ii) and the assumption that we should act in accordance with the principles of equality and respect embody value judgements, so we need to assess whether we should share these values. We will consider this under 9 and 10 below when we discuss general principles.

To evaluate the reasons upon which reason (iii) depends, we must consider whether it is true that the law against homosexual acts before the age of 21 did deter young men from reporting unwanted sexual advances. This is very difficult to judge, because it is difficult to gather positive evidence that someone has been deterred from doing something. Perhaps the most that the author needs to establish is that the law does nothing to protect young men from unwanted sexual advances. Again, this is difficult to judge. Perhaps some men who would like to make sexual advances to young men aged 16 to 21 are deterred from doing so by the law against homosexual acts under age 21. Another problem here is that even if, after a change in the law, we found more young men reporting unwanted advances, we would not know whether this was due to an increased willingness to make the reports (because the aspect of criminality had been removed), or to an increased number of unwanted advances being made. Perhaps we just have to remain open minded on this, in which case we can agree that those who wish to discriminate have not shown beyond doubt that discrimination with regard to the age of consent does have the practical benefit of protecting young men from unwanted sexual advances. The author is, of course, right that if the age of consent were lowered to 16, then boys would still have the same legal protection as girls from unwanted sexual advances, on the grounds that sex is illegal if consent is withheld. Or, at least, there would be the same legal protection in principle. It is possible that, in practice, boys' complaints might be treated less seriously than those of girls.

It is also difficult to evaluate the truth of reason (iv). It seems reasonable to accept that, if young gay men need to be contacted individually in order to get the message through to them about safe sex, and if they are afraid to acknowledge their homosexuality through fear of facing charges, then it would be easier to get the message across if the age of consent were lowered. We need to ask two questions here:

Do young gay men need to be contacted individually in order to get the message through to them about safe sex?

Are young gay men afraid to acknowledge their homosexuality through fear of facing charges?

In answer to the first question, perhaps general publicity would have as much effect as seeking out individuals. Do health workers seek out heterosexuals as well to give them messages about the risk of Aids, or do they rely on general publicity?

In answer to the second question, it is possible that the unwillingness of young gay men to talk to health workers about their sexuality is due not to fear of criminal charges, but to reluctance to admit to being gay in a society in which many (as the author acknowledges) still disapprove of homosexuality. If the author had raised this point, she might perhaps have pointed out that lowering the age of consent could possibly help to change such attitudes.

The point about consistency in relation to reason (v) is true, in that it cannot be someone's age *alone* which makes informed consent to homosexual acts impossible for those aged under 18. If you say that the reason why a young man is incapable of informed consent to homosexual acts is because he is under 18, then you must either accept that someone under 18 is incapable of informed consent to any sexual act, or say what is the difference between homosexual and heterosexual acts which shows that informed consent to the latter is possible for under 18s whereas informed consent to the former is not. The author aims to show that there is no such difference by stating that all the medical evidence shows that sexuality is settled before age 18. Again, it is difficult to assess the truth of this statement. Perhaps the author can rely simply on the observation that those who claim that there is a difference have not shown us what the difference is.

Not much direct evidence is given to support the claim in reason (vi) – that homosexuality is not a disease. But there seem to be no good reasons why we should think of it as a disease. It appears to be a characteristic which some men have throughout their lives, which is true of many diseases. But it also appears to be resistant to attempts to change it in an individual, which is untrue of many diseases, both mental and physical.

Moreover, any suffering experienced by the individual appears to be due to the disapproving attitudes of others, which is untrue of mental and physical disease.

It would be possible to check the details about ages of consent in other countries (reason (vii)), and there has been no publicity about problems resulting from ages of consent for homosexuals which are lower than the age of consent in Britain.

Reason (viii) is obviously true, in the sense that the recommended change in the law would ensure equality before the law. However, it is not certain that this change would ensure 'respect' for homosexuals.

The assumption that 16 is an appropriate age of consent for heterosexuals is reasonable, and tends not to be challenged even by those who favour a higher age of consent for homosexuals.

4 *Reliability of authorities*
The argument does not rely to any great extent on evidence from authorities. It mentions the author's gay friends who claim that they have always been attracted to the same sex. There is no reason to question the reliability of this claim.

It mentions 'sober, intelligent countries' which have lower ages of consent for homosexuals than does Britain. There is no reason to doubt that these countries base their policies on serious debate and evaluation of the relevant arguments.

5 *Additional evidence*
No relevant additional evidence comes to mind.

6 *Drawing further conclusions*
No obvious conclusions can be drawn from the passage, apart from the applications of principles which will be discussed under note 10.

7 *Explanations*
There is one explanation in the passage. The fact that Aids death figures are probably lower than everyone predicted is explained as due to the decision to seek out and advise young homosexuals who were seriously breaking the law. The point of the discussion in the third paragraph is to show that advice on safe sex can be effective, and that advice would be easier to give if criminality was not involved. The explanation is intended to show that advice on safe sex was effective in the mid-1980s, in that it reduced the numbers of deaths from Aids. The numbers of deaths from Aids may have been lower than predicted because the predictions were unrealistic, rather than because the messages about safe sex were effec-

tive. But for the purposes of the argument, the author only needs to convince us that trying to get over the message about safe sex is a good policy, and we can accept this even if we are not convinced that the lower than expected deaths figures are due to the policy. We can accept it because it is reasonable to think that such a policy could save *some* lives. So the plausibility of this particular explanation is not absolutely crucial to the argument.

8 *Analogies or comparisons*

The text makes comparisons in two areas – between young homosexuals and young heterosexuals, and between Britain and other countries.

The first of these comparisons is appropriate. If the only difference between two 17-year-olds is that one is homosexual and the other is heterosexual, then why should we not think that the two are alike in their ability to make informed choices about engaging in sexual acts?

The countries with which Britain is compared are similar to Britain in many respects, e.g. they are developed countries, democracies, and there is no reason to think that they have less concern for the welfare of their young people. There are differences of religion, but it is interesting to note that Ireland, a Catholic country, has set the age of consent for homosexuals at 17. It is appropriate to compare Britain with these countries, and suggest that if they have no problems with an equal age of consent, then Britain should not have problems either.

9 *Principles*

The argument relies on principles concerned with equality and respect. The principle of equality is made explicit in the statement:

> 'In a free society, the onus is on those who discriminate to explain its practical benefits.'

This means that people should be treated equally, unless some good is done by treating some people in a different way from others. In this example, homosexuals and heterosexuals should be treated equally with regard to the age of consent, unless there is some benefit to be gained from discriminating against homosexuals, e.g. protection of the young from unwanted homosexual advances. What other applications of this principle can we think of? It would imply that different ethnic groups should have exactly the same educational opportunities, unless there is some benefit to be gained from, for example, giving previously disadvantaged groups some extra privileges. It would mean that, for example, males and females should have equal opportunities to be selected as parliamentary candidates, unless there is some benefit to be gained from allowing only women to be on a short list for selection of a candidate. Some people would argue that the practical benefits of discrimination can never justify treating people unequally, because that would be to *use* individuals for the good of others. However, the author does not say that if there are practical benefits, one must discriminate. She merely insists that those who advocate discrimination must show what its benefits are. She may believe that the benefits of discrimination have to be enormous in order to justify it, and she may believe that, in order to be justified, these benefits have to be for the good of those discriminated against. The principle, expressed as it is, seems reasonable.

The idea of 'respect' is not mentioned explicitly until the last paragraph. Yet, in other parts of the passage, there are references to the young man of 17 being capable of giving informed consent, and to the idea that the personal judgement of gay men about their sex lives is dangerous, or not to be trusted, being 'absolute nonsense'. So underlying the discussion, there seems to be a principle which says that adults' judgements about how to run their own lives should be respected. Since we would each like our own decisions to be respected, we are unlikely to disagree with this principle, though it would, of course, have to be modified with the additional clause 'provided that their actions harm no-one else'. Some would also want it to be modified to read 'adults who are capable of making rational choices'. This modified principle will read:

> For all adults who are capable of making rational choices, we should respect their judgements about how to run their own lives, provided their actions do not harm others.

This principle strengthens the argument by implying something about the *way* in which people should be treated, thus adding to the point about equality. It is not just that homosexuals and heterosexuals should be treated equally; it is also that both should be treated as being capable of making informed choices about their sexuality.

10 *Strength of support for conclusion*

The passage produces a strong argument for an equal age of consent for homosexuals and heterosexuals, based on the principle that people should be treated equally unless discrimination can be shown to have benefits, together with the claim that this particular discrimination has not been shown to have the benefit it is supposed to have of protecting young men from unwanted advances.

The principle about respecting people's choices reinforces the view that it is inappropriate for the State to interfere in people's lives in the area of sexual orientation.

The point about advice on safe sex being easier to give if the age of consent for homosexuals were lower adds a little support, by showing that there *might* be some positive benefit from a lower age of consent, in addition to the benefit of equality of treatment.

The case for the common age of consent being 16 is not explored to any great extent. Currie claims that sexuality is settled before 18, which is meant to support the view that it is acceptable for the age of consent to be below 18. She mentions countries with common ages of consent ranging from 14 to 17, but does not consider which of these ages, if any, is the 'right' one. No doubt she takes it for granted that most people accept that in Britain 16 is the right age for heterosexual consent, and she is principally concerned with showing that homosexuals should be treated equally.

Example 2: Moralists – Richard D. North

(The paragraphs are numbered here, because the analysis refers to particular paragraphs.)

1   The International Fund for Animal Welfare's (IFAW) full-page advertisements in the broadsheet newspapers are stiff-arming Sir Ian MacLaurin, the chairman of Tesco, because that firm sells Canadian salmon. The argument goes that if he boycotts the salmon, the Canadian government will stop the seal-bashing on its ice-floes.

2   However, it so happens that the seals in question are thousands of miles from the salmon we are asked to resist eating. It is also probable that a salmon's death from 'drowning' in air is more horrible than a seal's having its brain stove in. Not one in a thousand of the T-shirt moralists who respond to IFAW's shock tactics will know or care about such fine-tuned matters.

3   And yet it is not on those grounds alone that I loathe this campaign. Nor is it merely that consumer boycotts are (forgive me) usually a rather blunt instrument. It may be right to call for a boycott of a nation's products in order to stop some horror in that country. Conceivably one should not buy Nike shoes because they are made by cheap labour in Asia (though I fear the cheap labourers might not agree).

4   Possibly it is right to try to halt the French nuclear testing by refusing to buy

the country's claret (though the French claret industry has enough problems with competition from heroically moral countries such as Australia and Chile). It may even be right to try to change the regime in Nigeria by boycotting Shell (though one fancies a Shell withdrawal would lead to worse environmental damage in the Niger delta).

5   IFAW's campaign goes beyond these ploys by asserting that Tesco (as opposed to the Tesco consumer) ought to make a moral choice about where to buy salmon. Worse, it also stigmatises the hapless Sir Ian. This latter problem looks partly to be his own fault: the advertisements quote him as saying in 1984 that the company should stand up and be counted (on what was actually a different issue), and so IFAW now appears to be asking for a degree of consistency from him.

6   Both practically and ethically, I am afraid that firms should never claim to be capable of being a force for good. And they certainly should not offer to censor products on behalf of consumers. That way lies the closure of almost all business and also an unwarranted control of customer choice.

7   Firms cannot pay the kind of wages some moralists might argue for; they cannot be as green as Greenpeace would like; they cannot be as virtuous in picking their trading partners overseas as civil rights campaigners would like. Firms operate in a morally and ecologically dubious world. Not merely are they often ill-placed to make the required judgements: provided they do not hide what they do, and where, it is someone else's business altogether to decide whether they should be allowed to trade in a particular way.

8   Firms can only hope to be decent citizens, and in their case that comes down to obeying the law. Firms make profits, governments make rules: that is a respectable ordering of things. What stinks about this advertisement is not that it may be a wrong-headed call for a consumer boycott. The creepiness much more consists in making a pariah of an individual who, were he to obey every exhortation of every pressure group, would have empty shelves, from which it follows that we would probably have empty larders.

9   I hope that Sir Ian enjoys his knighthood, and will heed a warning that going for a halo as well would be dangerous. More widely, the boss class in firms ought to think carefully before allowing their public relations people to fashion caring, goody-goody images for their enterprises: virtue is not something to be traded in.

(*Independent*, 20 November 1995)

Let us apply the method of assessment to this passage, which is quite a difficult one to analyse. Because of this, we start with a general summary of what is going on in the article.

Although there is evidence of emotive persuasion in this passage – for example, the reference to those whose view the author criticises as 'T-shirt moralists' – nevertheless some reasoning is being presented in order to convince us that, both practically and ethically, firms should never claim to be capable of being a force for good.

The reasoning for this conclusion appears from the sixth paragraph onwards. Before that there is some discussion as to whether it is ever right for consumers to boycott a nation's products, but the conclusions here are tentative. In the second paragraph there is also some criticism of the International Fund for Animal Welfare's (IFAW) reasoning.

Let's look first at this criticism. The author sets out the IFAW's argument as follows:

> *Reason (IFAW)*: If Tesco boycotts Canadian salmon, the Canadian government will stop the seal-bashing on its ice-floes.

Therefore:

> *Conclusion*: Tesco should boycott Canadian salmon.

The author's criticisms of this argument are as follows:

> (i) the seals in question are thousands of miles from the salmon.

If this is meant to cast doubt on the truth of the reason, it is not very effective. It would do so if the assumption behind the reason was that those who were killing seals depended on the sale of salmon for their livelihood. But the assumption which lies behind the reason appears to be that the Canadian government will be so worried about the damage to the Canadian economy that it will take steps to ensure that seal-bashing does not happen. This assumption may be untrue, but the distance between the salmon and the seals has no relevance to its truth or falsity.

> (ii) it is also probable that a salmon's death from 'drowning' in air is more horrible than a seal's from having its brain stove in.

This is meant to suggest that the IFAW should be boycotting salmon on the grounds that salmon fishing is cruel, rather than in an attempt to stop cruelty to seals. Even if it is true that the salmon's death is more horrible than the seal's, this does not show that the IFAW should not be trying to stop seal-bashing. However, by suggesting that from the IFAW's own point of view, the wrong reason is being given for boycotting salmon, the author is casting aspersions on the IFAW's process of reasoning.

Now let us look at the third and fourth paragraphs. Here the author indicates that he is not against boycotts on principle. He does this by listing some of the issues in response to which it *may* be morally right to boycott a nation's products, even though in each case he suggests that such boycotts would either not have the desired result, or would have other undesirable results. Two of the examples are cases in which human rights are at stake (i.e. cheap labour in Asia, and the regime in Nigeria which, though the author doesn't actually say so, is oppressive). The other example is one in which the actions of another nation could be damaging to humans as well as animal life and the environment (i.e. French nuclear testing). What these examples have in common is the possibility of harm to humans, and the choice of such cases suggests that the author believes that only if human welfare is at stake should consumers boycott the products of another country.

1 *Conclusion*
We have already identified the conclusion of the reasoning from the sixth paragraph to the end of the passage as:

> Both practically and ethically, firms should never claim to be capable of being a force for good.

2 *Reasons and assumptions*
We can set out the reasoning from the sixth paragraph to the end of the passage as follows.
In paragraph six:

> *Reason 1:* If firms offer to censor products on behalf of consumers, almost all businesses will close.

> *Reason 2:* If firms offer to censor products on behalf of consumers, this will constitute an unwarranted control of customer choice.

These two reasons are offered in support of:

> *Intermediate conclusion 1:* Firms should not offer to censor products on behalf of consumers (for both practical and ethical reasons)

In paragraph seven:

Reason 3: Firms are often ill-placed to make the required judgements.

This is offered in support of both:

Intermediate conclusion 2: Firms cannot be as green as Greenpeace would like.

and:

Intermediate conclusion 3: Firms cannot be as virtuous in picking their trading partners overseas as civil rights campaigners would like.

In paragraph seven, we also find reason 4, which will be used in drawing the main conclusion:

Reason 4: Firms cannot pay the kind of wages some moralists might argue for.

In both paragraphs seven and eight, we find:

Reason 5: Firms make profits, governments make rules: that is a respectable ordering of things.

Reason 6: Firms can only hope to be decent citizens, and in their case that comes down to obeying the law.

These two reasons are offered jointly to support:

Intermediate conclusion 4: Provided firms do not hide what they do, and where, it is someone else's business altogether to decide whether they should be allowed to trade in a particular way.

The support for the main conclusion is offered jointly by intermediate conclusions 1, 2, 3 and 4 and reason 4, in the following way:

Intermediate conclusion 1: Firms should not offer to censor products on behalf of consumers (for both practical and ethical reasons)

and

Intermediate conclusion 2: Firms cannot be as green as Greenpeace would like.

and

> *Intermediate conclusion 3:* Firms cannot be as virtuous in picking their trading partners overseas as civil rights campaigners would like.

and

> *Reason 4:* Firms cannot pay the kind of wages some moralists might argue for.

and

> *Intermediate conclusion 4:* Provided firms do not hide what they do, and where, it is someone else's business altogether to decide whether they should be allowed to trade in a particular way.

Therefore:

> *Main conclusion:* Both practically and ethically, firms should never claim to be capable of being a force for good.

You may wish to regard the statement in the final paragraph as the main conclusion (i.e. 'More widely, the boss class in firms ought to think carefully before allowing their public relations people to fashion caring, goody-goody images for their enterprises'), but this does not seem to go much further or be more important than the main conclusion identified above.

Now let's think about unstated assumptions.

One assumption has already been mentioned – that only if human welfare is at stake should consumers boycott the products of another country. However, this is not relevant to the main argument about what firms should or should not do.

Underlying reason 1 there is an assumption that if firms censor products, this will drastically affect their profits.

Underlying reason 2 there is an assumption that customers should have the widest possible choice of products.

Underlying reason 6 there is an assumption that there is no moral obligation on firms to influence governments to change laws or to introduce new laws.

3 *Truth of reasons and assumptions*

Reason 1 and its related assumption appear to make too extreme a claim. Surely firms could both boycott some products and remain in business.

Reason 2 and its related assumption are questionable. Why is it so important for customers to have the widest possible choice? Is this more important than, for example, for firms to take a stand on human rights?

Reason 3 seems to be suggesting that firms are often ill-placed to make judgements about environmental damage caused by producing certain goods, or to judge whether foreign governments are oppressive. This may be true, but the issue is usually about what they should do when they do have the relevant information.

Reason 4 may be true of some firms, which may go out of business if they paid very high wages.

Reason 5 seems acceptable – but most 'moralists' are not arguing that firms should take over the government's function of making rules.

Reason 6 and its related assumption are questionable. Being a 'decent citizen' could require more than merely obeying the law – it could require both firms and individuals to speak out against unjust laws and practices.

4 *Reliability of authorities*

The author does not appeal to any authorities to support his reasoning. He does attempt to undermine our trust in the IFAW's authority, by suggesting that those who demonstrate on their behalf are both ignorant and are not reasoning well.

5 *Additional evidence*

What additional evidence might have an impact on the argument? Some firms do make moral choices on behalf of their customers. We need to know in what way the profits of such firms have been affected. It is possible that public opinion is against 'seal-bashing', and that the public would be all the more eager to shop at a supermarket chain which took a moral stand. A survey of public opinion on this issue could have some impact on the argument.

6 *Drawing further conclusions*

No obvious conclusions can be drawn from the passage.

7 *Explanations*

No explanations were identified in the text.

8 *Analogies*

No comparisons are used in the reasoning.

9 *Principles*

The assumption underlying reason 2 embodies the principle that firms should not control customer choice. Does this mean that every firm should offer every available product? This would be unrealistic, so it must be seen as acceptable for a firm to control consumer choice in its own interest. Why, then, is it unwarranted for a firm to control consumer choice for ethical reasons?

The conclusion of the argument involves the principle that firms should not aim to act ethically. This suggests that they have no obligation, for example, to control pollution which may affect people's health, nor any obligation to try to persuade governments to introduce legislation on pollution. This seems unacceptable. Surely we should accept the moral principle that firms should not make a profit from making people suffer.

10 *Strength of support for conclusion*

The principal problem in the argument to intermediate conclusion 1 is that the truth of the reasons is dubious.

The same is true of the argument to intermediate conclusions 2 and 3.

The weakness of these sections of the argument means that great weight falls on intermediate conclusion 4. But the main conclusion is not well supported by intermediate conclusion 4. One reason for this is that the scope of the main conclusion is too wide – it implies not just that firms should not boycott products, but also that they should have no concern about directly causing harm in their pursuit of profit. The other reason is that intermediate conclusion 4 establishes only that firms do not have the legal obligation to try to be a force for good, beyond obeying the laws. It does not follow from this that they should never attempt to be a force for good.

Exercise 4 Assessing longer passages of reasoning

Now try for yourself to analyse and assess the reasoning in the following passages. Make a note of any ethical concepts upon which the reasoning relies.

1 When it is right to destroy nature

Nicholas Schoon

One of Britain's rarest fungi is found only in the dung of New Forest ponies. Several colleagues greeted this information with derision when my little article about plans to conserve this species, the nail fungus, appeared in Monday's *Independent*. Why bother? It is a fair question: today the Government publishes plans to conserve the diversity of Britain's plants and animal species.

Most of us can feel quite passionate about the harm that humanity's persecution or recklessness has done to the charismatic otter, red squirrel or golden eagle. But who, beyond a few dozen specialists in museums and university biology departments, really cares about the hundreds of small, utterly obscure plant and animal species in Britain that are declining or are endangered because of our activities? Why should we make sacrifices or spend money on their behalf?

If you believe in a divine Creation, then answers are easy. We have no right to wipe out what God made. If you are an atheist, you can argue that we have a powerful self-interest in slowing the great wave of man-made extinctions now gathering pace all over the world. You would say that we have discovered thousands of useful products such as drugs and food additives in wild species, and, of course, all our farm animals and crops come from the wild. We continue to find new uses for species or chemicals within them –why damn this stream by wiping them out?

But for me, all the best arguments are moral and aesthetic ones. Many greens talk about the billions of species on earth living in harmony in the great web of life, and the planetary dangers of upsetting a fragile balance. This is actually unscientific bunkum; the *Lion King* view of nature. A genuine ecologist will tell you that ecosystems are in constant flux rather than balance. While species can have extraordinarily complex and co-operative relationships, for the most part their interactions are utterly ruthless and consist of eating or being eaten.

Nature seems very careless with its own. For the billions of years during which life on earth has existed, individual species have been continuously disappearing. Existing species or entirely new ones soon take their place. But there is enormous creativity and complexity emerging from the ceaseless struggle –you only have to find ou t a little about a coral reef, a mangrove swamp or an ancient European wood-land to understand this. Environmentalists say the destruction of any species by mankind is the equivalent to burning a precious, ancient book in a vast library. Wiping out an ecosystem is akin to demolishing a medieval cathedral.

These are powerful images, but I cannot see any connection. Wild habitats and the mind-boggling diversity of species in the sea, on the land and in the air (there are tens of thousands in Britain alone) were created by blind, utterly impersonal forces such as changes in climate, earlier mass extinctions and evolution.

Even so, the most rudimentary understanding of the processes involved leads you straight to the realisation that each species is special, however boring, ugly and even unpleasant it may appear to us. It has its own uniqueness, it own place, its own history, which is of a different order to the boring, trivial uniqueness of each separate grain of sand on a beach. Once you accept that, the fluffy animal approach to wildlife conservation seems barbaric, irrational. Why should red squir-rels and golden eagles and beautiful butterflies get all the attention merely because a majority of humans think they are cute?

If we are rational and care to understand the natural world we uneasily live in, then every wild being threatened by mankind's economic and population growth deserves equal conservation efforts from us –including the lowly nail fungus.

There are exceptions –species such as smallpox and the tsetse fly which cause serious suffering and death to people. We have the right to eliminate those entirely, provided that in doing so we do not endanger entire ecosystems and ourselves (which is what happened with DDT).

If every species is unique and of equal value, what gives us that right? Two reasons. Homo sapiens is by far the most interesting and important species on the planet –like it or not we are lords o f nature.

And in choosing to wage war on our natural enemies, we are only playing by nature's own rules.

(*Independent*, 15 May 1996)

2 Viciousness for voyeurs

Mary Midgley

Is boxing still a sport? Is it any more objectionable than other things that do still count as sport? There are, of course, lots of interesting sporting ways in which one can get killed or injured, such as mountain climbing or hang gliding. But people who do these things do them on their own hook, not in the process of helping to kill someone else. They are not paid for doing it, nor are there crowds of spectators watching them do it. Their friends and relatives may object to them doing it, and that can perhaps be properly regarded as a matter for private negotiation, like other dangerous choices. It is not weighted by the offer of substantial pay from the watchers.

People can also get killed in sports that are not ranked as specially dangerous, such as riding or football. But this is recognised as contrary to the intention and spirit of the sport. It is, indeed, a bit bizarre that armour is now needed for games such as cricket. There have been suggestions that sports ought not to need armour. But most sensible people involved seem now to reason that, when balls are moving fast enough to kill you, wearing armour accords better with the spirit of the game than being dead or brain damaged does. Similarly, deaths in steeplechasing have led to modifications in the courses. And so on in other sports.

So what is different about boxing? Among the sports that we now allow, it is the only one where physical injury is essential. Knocking your opponent out is central to it, and we now know that every knock-out leaves lasting damage to the brain. Blows short of knock-outs also do much damage, though more gradually. Boxing and wrestling, unlike all other sports, isolate the elements of direct physical combat; they cannot be won except by literally beating the adversary. Wrestling is not now in question because it does not seem recently to have led to fatalities. Perhaps, as we are led to believe, it is all fixed anyway; perhaps its rules are better. But anyway, it does not concentrate on the head. And we now know enough about the human head to be sure that knocking it about is not a reasonable sporting activity.

This piece of scientific information about heads and their contents is one thing that divides our age from past ones and gives us reason to find boxing more objectionable than they did. But perhaps an even more important difference is our changed attitude to physical injury and suffering in general.

In nearly all past ages, people took frequent pain and danger as a matter of course, and lived with it all their days. The spectators at an Elizabethan bear-baiting were people who themselves had their teeth drawn, or, when necessary, their legs amputated, without anaesthetics. Similarly, the bystanders at an 18th century boxing match were largely people used to defending themselves with their own fists on occasion.

By contrast, the spectators at present-day boxing matches are mainly people who would not themselves willingly have a tooth stopped without an anaesthetic, and would not have the first idea what to do if they had to fight for their lives. If they were brain damaged in the course of their work, they'd expect to sue. Of course, our current freedom from pain is an enormous advantage. But its effect for sports like boxing is a most unpleasant shift in the motives available to the spectators – a shift away from genuine, practical fellow feeling in a shared skill towards sadistic, voyeuristic fantasy.

These are disagreeable words, and they do not, of course, only apply to boxing. A great deal of TV entertainment shares this kind of corruption. There is something just as false and voyeuristic about the fashion for filmed car chases and car crashes, because here too the actual experiences of the victims are suppressed in an unreal excitement about the processes of destruction themselves. (It is likely enough, as has been suggested, that the 'joy riding' which led to death and played a part in the recent riots springs from this kind of addiction.) In boxing, however, the physical effects are not suppressed but are central to the experience in a way that they are not in any other sport, and they are known to be such as will gradually destroy the participants.

By contrast, the Japanese have evolved a number of highly skilled martial arts which are designed to avoid injuring those who practise them. If the boxing public wants some form of formal duelling to persist, and wants to claim that its motives for doing so are impeccable, perhaps this is the direction in which it will have to move. In any case, we have surely had enough of boxing.

(*Guardian*, 24 September 1991)

3 Confronting our own mortality

Melanie Phillips

It is easy to be swept along by an emotional response to the conviction of Dr. Nigel Cox for the attempted murder of his patient, Mrs. Lillian Boyes. Mrs. Boyes died after Dr. Cox, a rheumatologist, injected her with two ampoules of potassium chloride. Repeated doses of heroin had failed to control her pain from acute rheumatoid arthritis complicated by gastric ulcers, gangrene and body sores. The sheer scale of her suffering and the indisputable caring impulse that drove Dr. Cox to take the action he did resulted in the deep distress of the jury when they returned their verdict, a distress quickly translated into outrage among spectators in the courtroom and far beyond.

Branding a doctor a criminal is deeply shocking when he has undoubtedly acted in what he thought were the best interests of his dying patient –especially when Mrs. Boyes herself had asked to be put out of her misery. Such a case preys upon our deeply-rooted fears about our own mortality and the manner of our own deaths; we tend to recoil, shuddering, from the public disgrace of a doctor for managing this particular death in what he thought was the right way. But we have to stand back from such emotions. We have to ask the difficult questions. Was Doctor Cox actually right to act as he did, and did he have any alternative to doing it?

Both prosecuting authorities and juries will usually seize on any legal lifelines thrown to them to help avoid either a prosecution or a conviction in cases of mercy killing. Had Dr. Cox injected Mrs. Boyes with an analgesic which incidentally hastened her death, the jury would probably not have convicted him. This is because the law permits treatment intended to relieve suffering, even if it carries the risk of accelerating death. It is against the law, however, to administer a drug with the *intention* of causing or hastening death. Potassium chloride has no analgesic properties. Its effect, as every medical student knows, is to stop a person's heart from beating. The jury well understood this crucial distinction. Their verdict showed that, despite some fudging of the issue by the defence, they believed Dr. Cox had done what he did specifically to end Mrs. Boyes' life.

So was this the right action to take? Was this, as the defence claimed, the only course open to him since all attempts to control her pain had failed? And should the law be changed as a result? This is an area where apparently hair's-breadth distinctions are utterly crucial. It has been said that doctors up and down the land are quietly doing what Dr. Cox did; the only difference was that he unwisely used a particular drug which ensnared him in the law; if only he'd used something else he wouldn't have been caught. But on the contrary, all the evidence is that only a few doctors have actively killed their patients. Doctors do withhold life-prolonging treatment where someone is clearly and irreversibly dying, to allow them to die with as much dignity as possible. And they do also administer pain relief which might have the side-effect of hastening the death of an already dying patient.

But there is a significant moral difference between ensuring that the natural process of dying is made as comfortable as possible, and actively precipitating someone's death by artificial means. The former is absolutely in line with a doctor's commitments to preserve life and relieve suffering; the other is not. The crux of the difference lies in the intention behind the act. It cannot be right for doctors to count death as one of their range of treatments to relieve suffering; it would turn them into a profession of benign executioners.

It is also not necessary. The essence of Dr. Cox's case was that Mrs. Boyes' pain was so severe it was resistant to all pain-relief. Yet it is not clear that all pain-relief avenues *were* exhausted. There was no evidence, for example, that any experts in palliative medicine were called to Mrs. Boyes' bed-side. Other rheumatologists gave evidence that the pain was untreatable, but rheumatologists are not experts in pain-relief. Moreover, a dying person's pain is inextricably mixed up with the anguish of dying. By and large, hospital staff are untrained and ill-equipped, both in their clinical skills *and* their own emotional responses, to treat the dying patient appropriately. Hospice staff constantly receive terminally ill patients from hospitals where they have suffered grave mental and physical distress because hospital staff cannot cope easily with the needs of the dying. But by their skilled care, hospice staff manage to make the life that remains worth living again. Terminal pain relief is a specialised skill; using death as a means of pain relief is a failure of medical care. And in extremis, as Dr. Robert Twycross, Clinical Reader in Palliative Medicine at Oxford, wrote to the Independent yesterday, administering heavy sedation until death occurs relieves suffering while respecting life itself.

The Cox case is held to have accelerated the cause of legalising voluntary euthanasia. One of the worries about voluntary euthanasia is that it can easily slide into mercy killing without the patient's consent and so into abuse. Philosophers tend to deride the slippery slope argument, but as so often they thus show themselves to be hopelessly out of touch with real life. As Dr. Twycross wrote, this slide into abuse is already happening in the Netherlands, where informal passive euthanasia is permitted. Here in Britain, the Abortion Act is a good example of the moral slippery slope in action; whatever one thinks about the rights and wrongs of abortion, its current scale and scope surely lay far beyond the intentions of Sir David Steel when he introduced his reforming bill back in the sixties. Bring in voluntary euthanasia, and we'll soon be asking questions such as: how do we define intolerable suffering? What is informed consent when a person is in the final stages of terminal illness? and so forth. People have the right to kill themselves. That doesn't mean that they have the right to expect others to assist them.

Some people thought the trial judge, Mr. Justice Ognall, was too harsh when he said Dr. Cox's conduct was not only criminal but a total betrayal of his unequivocal duty as a physician. The trouble was that it was. There are those who think that if they ever wanted to commit suicide, they'd like a doctor to help them. But it is of over-riding importance that the population as a whole can absolutely trust that their doctors won't kill them.

Death is the great modern taboo. The neglect of terminal care, the paucity of hospices and the lack of training for doctors and nurses in the care of the dying reflects our unwillingness, in a society geared to instant gratification, to confront our own mortality. It would be a travesty if the priority we now decide to afford to the dying is to get rid of them more quickly through euthanasia. We should resist this kind of utilitarian brutality. Instead, we should be bending our efforts to preventing the kind of suffering endured by Mrs. Boyes and protecting the human dignity of natural death.

(*Guardian*, 25 September 1992)

4 An extract from 'A Defense of Abortion'

Judith Jarvis Thomson

I propose.that we grant that the fetus is a person from the mom ent of conception. How does the argument go from here? Something like this, I take it. Every person has a right to life. So the fetus has a right to life. No doubt the mother has a right to decide what shall happen in and to her body; everyone would grant that. But surely a person's right to life is stronger and more stringent than the mother's right to decide what happens in and to her body, and so outweighs it. So the fetus may not be killed; an abortion may not be performed.

It sounds plausible. But now let me ask you to imagine this. You wake up in the morning and find yourself back to back in bed with an unconscious violinist. A famous unconscious violinist. He has been found to have a fatal kidney ailment, and the Society of Music Lovers has canvassed all the available medical records and found that you alone have the right blood type to help. They have therefore kidnapped you, and last night the violinist's circulatory system was plugged into yours, so that your kidneys can be used to extract poisons from his blood as well as your own. The director of the hospital now tells you 'Look, we're sorry the Society of Music Lovers did this to you – we would never have permitted it if we had known. But still, they did it, and the violinist is now plugged into you. To unplug you would be to kill him. But never mind, it's only for nine months. By then he will have recovered from his ailment, and can safely be unplugged from you.' Is it morally incumbent on you to accede to this situation? No doubt it would be very nice of you if you did, a great kindness. But do you *have* to accede to it? What if it were not nine months, but nine years? Or longer still? What if the director of the hospital says 'Tough luck, I agree, but you've now got to stay in bed, with the violinist plugged into you, for the rest of your life. Because remember this. All persons have a right to life, and violinists are persons. Granted you have a right to decide what happens in and to your body, but a person's right to life outweighs your right to decide what happens in and to your body. So you cannot ever be unplugged from him.' I imagine you would regard this as outrageous, which suggests that something really is wrong with that plausible-sounding argument I mentioned a moment ago.

In this case, of course, you were kidnapped; you didn't volunteer for the operation that plugged the violinist into your kidneys. Can those who oppose abortion on the ground I mentioned make an exception for a pregnancy due to rape? Certainly. They can say that persons have a right to life only if they didn't come into existence because of rape; or they can say that all persons have a right to life, but that some have less of a right to life than others, in particular, that those who come into existence because of rape have less. But these statements have a rather unpleasant sound. Surely the question of whether you have a right to life at all, or how much of it you have, shouldn't turn on the question of whether or not you are the product of a rape. And in fact the people who oppose abortion on the ground I mentioned do not make this distinction, and hence do not make an exception in the case of rape.

Nor do they make an exception for a case in which the mother has to spend the nine months of her pregnancy in bed. They would agree that would be a great pity, and hard on the mother; but all the same, all persons have a right to life, and the fetus is a person, and so on. I suspect, in fact, that they would not make an exception for a case in which, miraculously enough, the pregnancy went on for nine years, or even the rest of the mother's life.

Some won't even make an exception for a case in which continuation of the pregnancy is likely to shorten the mother's life; they regard abortion as impermissible even to save the mother's life. Such cases are nowadays very rare, and many opponents do not accept this extreme view. All the same, it is a good place to begin: a number of points of interest come out in respect to it.

Let us call the view that abortion is impermissible even to save the mother's life 'the extreme view'. I want to suggest first that it does not issue from the argument I mentioned earlier without the addition of some fairly powerful premises. Suppose a woman has become pregnant, and now learns that she has a cardiac condition such that she will die if she carries the baby to term. What may be done for her? The fetus, being a person, has a right to life, but as the mother is a person too, so has she a right to life. Presumably they have an equal right to life. How is it supposed to come out that an abortion may not be performed? If mother and child have an equal right to life, shouldn't we perhaps flip a coin? Or should we add to the mother's right to life her right to decide what happens in and to her body, which everybody seems to be ready to grant – the sum of her rights now outweighing the fetus' right to life?

The most familiar argument here is the following. We are told that performing the abortion would be directly killing the child, whereas doing nothing would not be killing the mother, but only letting her die. Moreover in killing the child, one would be killing an innocent person, for the child has committed no crime, and is not aiming at his mother's death…

If directly killing an innocent person is murder, and thus is impermissible, then the mother's directly killing the innocent person inside her is murder, and thus is impermissible. But it cannot seriously be thought to be murder if the mother performs an abortion on herself to save her life. It cannot seriously be said that she *must* refrain, that she *must* sit passively by and wait for her death. Let us look again at the case of you and the violinist. There you are, in bed with the violinist, and the director of the hospital says to you, 'It's all most distressin g, and I deeply sympathize, but you see this is putting an additional strain on your kidneys, and you'll be dead within the month. But you *have* to stay where you are all the same. Because unplugging you would be directly killing an innocent violinist, and that's murder, and that's impermissible". If anything in the world is true, it is that you do not commit murder, you do not do what is impermissible, if you reach around to your back and unplug yourself from that violinist to save your life.

The main focus of attention in writings on abortion has been on what a third party may or may not do in answer to a request from a woman for an abortion. This is in a way understandable. Things being as they are, there isn't much a woman can safely do to abort herself. So the question asked is what a third party may do, and what the mother may do, if this is mentioned at all, is deduced, almost as an afterthought, from what it is concluded that third parties may do. But it seems to me that to treat the matter in this way is to refuse to grant to the mother that very status of person which is so firmly insisted on for the fetus. For we cannot simply read off what a person may do from what a third party may do. Suppose you find yourself trapped in a tiny house with a growing child. I mean a very tiny house, and a rapidly growing child –you are already up against the wall of the hous e and in a few minutes you'll be crushed to death. The child on the other hand won't be crushed to death; if nothing is done to stop him from growing he'll be hurt, but in the end he'll simply burst open the house and walk out a free man. Now I could well understand it if a bystander were to say, "There's nothing we can do for you. We cannot choo se between your life and his, we cannot be the ones to decide who is to live, we cannot intervene". But it cannot be concluded that you too can do nothing, that you cannot attack it to save your life. However innocent the child may be, you do not have to wait passively while it crushes you to death. Perhaps a pregnant woman is vaguely felt to have the status of house, to which we don't allow the right of self-defence. But if the woman houses the child, it should be remembered that she is a person who houses it.

I should perhaps stop to say explicitly that I am not claiming that people have a right to do anything whatever to a save their lives. I think, rather, that there are drastic limits to the right of self-defence. If someone threatens you with death unless you torture someone else to death, I think you have not the right, even to save your life, to do so. But the case under consideration here is very different. In our case there are only two people involved, one whose life is threatened, and one who threatens it. Both are innocent: the one who is threatened is not threatened because of any fault, the one who threatens does not threaten because of any fault. For this reason we may feel that we bystanders cannot intervene. But the person threatened can.

In sum, a woman can surely defend her life against the threat posed to it by the unborn child, even if doing so involves its death. And this shows ..that the extreme view of abortion is false, and so we n eed not canvass any other possible ways of arriving at it from the argument I mentioned at the outset.

(Judith J. Thomson, 'A Defense of Abortion', *Philosophy and Public Affairs*, 1 (Fall 1971): 48–53. Copyright © 1971 by Princeton Universit y Press. Reprinted by permission of Princeton University Press)

5 Should those who abuse their bodies pay the price?

Glenda Cooper

'Disease generally begins that equality which death completes', said Samuel Johnson. But in the world of modern health care it seems some patients are now more equal than others.

The allegations made last week that a 15-year-old girl had been denied a liver transplant after taking ecstasy raised once again the moral question: if a patient is a smoker, a drinker or a drug abuser, does that somehow make them less worthy of treatment than virtuous people who have eaten their greens every day?

The details of Michelle Paul's case are not yet known, as the fatal accident inquiry has been adjourned until April, when Ms Paul's surgeon, Hilary Sanfrey, will have the chance to testify. But if it does emerge that Ms Paul was denied the chance of a liver transplant solely on 'moral grounds', because of her drug use, this will make us question anew the values that we apply when deciding who gets treatment.

Drug users are not the first people to fall foul of implicit rationing in the NHS. In the past there have been claims that smokers and drinkers have been left at the back of the queue. In 1993, Harry Elphick, 47, was refused treatment for a heart condition because he was a heavy smoker. Consultants at Wythenshawe hospital in Manchester told him that tests to show if a by-pass was needed were not carried out on smokers. Mr Elphick quit his 25-a-day habit, but died a week before he was due to see doctors again.

Then in 1995 it was reported that transplant units were under pressure to stop offering £60,000 liver transplants to alcoholics, after evidence from the US that most patients return to heavy drinking after the operation. By some criteria it seems a logical policy. The UK Transplant Support Services Authority reports that there was a 6,000 strong waiting list for all organ transplants at the beginning of 1996. By the end of the year, despite 2,750 taking place, the waiting list had grown by 5 per cent.

So why should the rest of us pay for a new heart for someone who has brought their condition upon themselves by puffing away on 40-a-day? Why should someone who regularly consumes three bottles of vodka a day – as Jim Baxter, the former Scottish football inter national who received two new livers, was said to do – receive a new org an after bringing cirrhosis upon themselves? This is, after all, the real world where there are never enough organs to go round and the dangers of excessive drinking or smoking have been clear for years.

But to start rationing because of deviant lifestyles is a dangerous step. The General Medical Council felt the need to make its view explicit in 1995 when it issued revised guidelines making it clear that doctors 'must not allow their views about a patient's lifestyle, culture, beliefs, race, colour, sex, sexuality, age, social status, or perceived economic worth to prejudice the treatment they give or arrange'. The council added that doctors 'must not refuse or delay treatment because [they] believe that patients' actions have contributed to their condition'. The British Medical Association said decisions must be made on clinical need and 'patients should not be discriminated against on the basis of moral judgements'.

Where, after all, do moral judgements leave us? There have also been allegations of discrimination and prejudice against drunk drivers, gay men with HIV, women seeking abortions, people from ethnic minorities and the elderly. In the end, should dentists refuse to treat children who have persistently and defiantly eaten sweets all their lives?

If a smoker, a drinker or a drug user is unlikely to survive a complicated transplant operation then, in the real world, it is better to give the organ to someone who can benefit more. But to condemn them purely for their habit and refuse to treat them on that basis is repulsive.

Surely it is more important to encourage more people to pledge their organs for use after their death so the waiting list can be contained, rather than stigmatising people for their habits. 'Life unworthy of life' was, after all, the phrase used by the Nazis to justify the murder of 100,000 psychiatric patients in the run-up to the Final Solution.

(*Independent*, 28 January 1997)

Chapter 4

Decision making

In the previous three chapters we have concentrated on analysing and assessing reasoning which has been presented by others. We should, of course, exercise the skills thus developed on our own reasoning as well as on other people's reasoning. However, we could become very skilled in criticism and self-criticism of this kind without ever attempting to resolve an ethical issue. Indeed, becoming very good at criticism can produce an unwillingness ever to come to a definite conclusion of one's own. We should remember that critical thinking involves judging what is good in reasoning as well as what is bad, and that the point of improving one's reasoning is to be able to form reasonable beliefs and to take appropriate action. If we want to become *effective* critical thinkers, we must be able and willing to make well-reasoned decisions of our own.

We all have to make decisions on a variety of issues – for example, which university to go to, which career to aim for, which car or which house to buy. Some of the decisions we make will have moral implications – for example, what kind of moral or religious education is right for our children, whether to care for elderly relatives at home, whether to break a law which we consider to be a bad law, how much to donate to charity. Some of these are major decisions –

more important than deciding what to wear when you get up in the morning, and they all involve some uncertainty. You can't be absolutely sure how they are going to turn out. However, this doesn't mean that there is no point in trying to make a good decision.

Before reading on, think for a moment about the best way to go about making a difficult decision. You could think about it in relation to a major decision which you have had to make in recent years. If it turned out well, was this just luck, or was it because of the way you made the decision? If it turned out badly, can you think of steps you should have taken which could have produced a better outcome? Before reading on, try to write a list of things you should have done in order to ensure that the decision had the best chance of turning out well.

One thing which will probably have occurred to you is that when making a decision, you need to be clear about what you can do – what *choices or options* are open to you. You then need to be able to work out the *implications or consequences* of each of these options, – you may ask yourself, for example, 'What will my life be like if I go to university A rather than university B, or if I defer the choice of university for another year and travel, or find employment?'. In the course of trying to answer these questions, you may find that you have to seek *information*, so that one important step in decision making must be to gather relevant information. When you have the information, and are able to envisage the possible consequences, you need to judge which set of consequences is preferable, to *evaluate* them. We have thus identified four important components of decision making – options, information, consequences and evaluation.

The optimising strategy

Each of these components is captured in one standard critical thinking model of decision making, a model most closely associated with the work of Bob Swartz (R. Swartz and S. Parks, *Infusing Critical and Creative Thinking into Content Instruction*, Pacific Grove, California, Critical Thinking Press and Software, 1992). It is called the optimising strategy because it requires us to aim for the best possible decision. Here is a version of the model, which we shall use in order to get started on making decisions.

Optimising strategy for decision making

1 Consider why a decision is necessary (is it necessary?).
2 List the options (i.e. the various possible courses of action).
3 For each option:

(a) list the consequences

(b) consider how likely are any consequences identified under 3(a) (take account of evidence and assess its reliability)

(c) consider how important the consequences are

(d) decide whether each of the listed consequences counts for or against the option.

4 Judge between the options in the light of your comments under 3(a)–(d)

Stage 1 in this model – thinking about why a decision is necessary – is something we have not yet mentioned, but it can be a useful preliminary to getting clear about priorities. More will be said about this when we have looked at some examples.

Stage 2 clearly relates to our earlier comments about the need to identify the options, and Stage 3(a) to our comment that we must work out the consequences of the options.

Stages 2, 3(a) and 3(b) may require the gathering of information, and it is at these stages that many of the skills you have already practised come into play. You will need to assess the reliability of any information which you acquire, to make explicit any assumptions which you are taking for granted, and to draw well-grounded conclusions about what kinds of consequences may result from a particular action, and how likely it is that those consequences will occur.

Stages 3(c), 3(d) and 4 involve evaluation as to which of the sets of consequences is the most desirable. In decisions about your personal life, it may not be too difficult to know what your preferences are, although in some cases you may have to choose between two possible outcomes, both of which seem desirable in some way. For example, when choosing a subject for study at university, you may wish to have an easy time, and be tempted to look for a course which will allow you to engage in many other activities. And yet, you may also be aware of the value in the long term of succeeding in a more challenging course. We could describe this as a competition between some immediate or short-term desires and some wider value, some more general view as to what matters in life, what is worthwhile. Often, the evaluation process in personal decisions will rest upon values of this kind.

Applying the optimising strategy

In order to illustrate the use of this strategy, we present below two cases for you to consider.

Example 1: The radiologist

A woman had a fatal reaction during urography. The radiologist indicated he did not warn this patient (or any other patients) of a possible fatal reaction to urography because it would not do any good.

'I could have told her', he said 'that there was a chance she might have a reaction and even die. After calming her down I would then have told her that she had seen two urologists in the past week and both of them had told her she needed urography. I have done 6,000 to 8,000 urograms in the past 13 years and no one has ever had a fatal reaction. We have been doing urograms at this hospital for at least 25 years and no one has ever had a fatal reaction. Because the indications for urography were great and the chances for a reaction were remote I am sure I would have convinced Mrs. E. to have the procedures. She would then have had the reaction and died and the fact that I warned her would have done Mrs. E. absolutely no good'.

The radiologist contended that the American College of Radiology should adopt the following policy: 'Our responsibility is to our patients and to do what is best for our patients medically. Informing patients of risks and possible death from urography may not be in the best interest of the patient and.it may be dangerous'.

(Beauchamp and Childress, *Principles of Biomedical Ethics*: pp. 291–2)

Imagine that you are the radiologist in this case, and use the optimising strategy in order to make a decision as to whether the patient should be told the risks of the procedure. You need to know that urography is not a treatment, but is an exploratory procedure which uses X-rays in order to find out whether someone has a serious condition which may need an operation – for example, whether a patient has cancer. In order to make your task easier, assume that what the radiologist says about the patient is true (i.e. that, given her symptoms, it was important that she should have a urogram), and that the figures he gives are accurate.

Here is another example for you to work through, before we discuss this case further.

Example 2

A childminder looks after six children for two hours every morning, and tries to ensure that each of them plays with toys of their choice. Sometimes when two want to play with the same toy, they will be able to share it. But the most popular toy, a tricycle, can be used by only one child at a time, and the childminder has to decide for how long each child can use it. She knows that five of the children would not complain if each child had an equal amount of time with the tricycle, but that the other child would fly into a tantrum if his time were limited, and would be aggressive towards the rest. She knows that one very timid child would make no fuss if he were not allowed to use the tricycle, even though he wants to. Because she wants harmony in the group, and wants most of the children to be happy, she is tempted to let the aggressive child have a longer period with the tricycle, and not to give the timid child any time at all with the tricycle.

Imagine that you are in the position of the childminder, and use the optimising strategy to decide what to do.

Comments on Example 1

These two examples are offered not in order to see if you can make the right decision, but in order to illustrate some special features of ethical decision making. So we shall not set out every step of the procedure, but instead make some broad comments about each case.

In response to Example 1, you may have agreed with the decision of the radiologist, and thought that the consequences were for the best if the patient were not told the risks of urography. Or you may have thought that his reasoning ignored something important, namely that it was not up to him to decide on behalf of a patient that a procedure with a risk, however small, should be carried out. But if he did leave out something important, where could he be said to have gone wrong in applying the optimising strategy? He thought about the consequences if he told the patient – that she was very unlikely to die, that she would have been very distressed if she had been told, that she may even have refused to undergo the procedure, which could have meant that she did not receive life-saving treatment. He compared this with the consequences if he did not tell her – that she was unlikely to die, that she would not be distressed about the procedure, and that she would agree to it, thereby making it more likely that she would get life-saving treatment. He judged that the consequences of the second option were better because they did not include distress for the patient caused by telling her about the risks.

We are not going to say whether he was right or wrong in this particular case, and perhaps one would need to know more about the patient's personality in order to do this. But there does seem to be something in the claim that one of the things he should have been aware of was that he was getting the patient's agreement to something without giving her the full facts, and that there will be cases where this would be the wrong thing to do. For example, surely it would be wrong to get someone to sign a consent form for an operation which had only a 50 per cent chance of success without telling the patient what the chance of success was. The assumption underlying such a claim is that most people are capable of making decisions about their own lives and that in general they should be allowed to do that, and should be given any information relevant to the decision. In this connection, we often find that the word 'autonomy' is used. 'Autonomy' can be defined as the capacity to make decisions for oneself, 'respecting autonomy' as allowing others the freedom to make decisions for themselves, and 'creating autonomy' as helping to put others in a position (perhaps by giving them information) to make decisions for themselves.

To be fair to the radiologist, perhaps he did think about autonomy, and yet in this instance, given that the risk of death was so small, placed a higher value on avoiding distress to the patient than on respecting her autonomy. However his justification does not mention autonomy, yet seems to apply the optimising strategy. We can learn two important things from these observations.

The first is that the optimising strategy might lead someone to overlook values such as autonomy, because it is possible to interpret the question 'What are the consequences of this option?' as meaning nothing more than 'What will happen if I do x?', even though one important aspect of the question may be 'What sort of description can be given of the action itself?' Perhaps you did think about the importance of autonomy in the case, even though you were using the optimising strategy, but we need to be sure that our decision-making model does not allow us to overlook important ethical considerations, so it would be a good idea to make these explicit in the model.

The second lesson from this example, prompted by the thought that the radiologist may have judged autonomy to be less important in this case than the avoidance of harm, is that when we are making decisions on ethical issues we may be faced with judging between competing values, just as we can be with decisions which affect only our own lives. But in the case of ethical decisions, it is not good enough to ask 'What *do* I value most?'. The appropriate question is 'What *should* I value most?' We shall return to this point about ethical values when we have commented on the second example.

Comments on Example 2

You may have had very little difficulty coming to the conclusion that the childminder should not yield to the temptation to allow the more disruptive child to have a greater share of time with the most desirable toy, even though this would ensure relative harmony within the group, and would reduce his aggression towards other children. If so, your assumption may have been that it would simply be unfair to the more timid child not to give him an equal share of time, and that any behaviour problems which this might cause in the more aggressive child would have to be dealt with in other ways. The value which you would be emphasising here would be that of justice, which can be defined as 'treating equals equally'. This is a value upon which we often rely when reasoning about moral issues – it underlies disapproval of racist and sexist behaviour, for example. Yet, as with Example 1, it would be possible to overlook this value when applying the optimising strategy, and simply to think about the consequences in terms of how contented the children were. The timid child would be disappointed, of course, but the aggressive child would be delighted, and the other five would not have to suffer his tantrums, so there may be more contentment than disappointment within the group. Yet it seems that justice or fairness is something which should be taken into account when making this decision.

General comments on the optimising strategy

Let us now turn to some more general comments about the role of values in ethical decision making. We have seen that we have to have some values in order to make a decision, otherwise there would be no way of judging between options. But we have also suggested that the proper question with ethical decisions is not 'What *do* I value?', but 'What *should* I value?' Does this leave us with no basis for making ethical decisions? No. We pointed out in Chapter 2 that the very process of ethical reasoning depends upon some basic moral responses, such as accepting that it is wrong to cause harm, so this is one value which does not need to be justified. We have now identified two other important values which should be taken into account when attempting to make a decision on an ethical issue. We do not have to ask 'What's so good about respecting autonomy?' or 'What's so good about trying to be just?' We know that these things are good. Of course, we may on occasions have to ask 'Is it more important in this case to respect autonomy or to minimise distress?', and such questions will be difficult to answer. But we shall not have made a good decision if we have overlooked questions about autonomy and justice. You may think that to have your autonomy over-ruled and to be treated unjustly are simply aspects of harm, rather than separate categories, and this is a reasonable point of view. But we wish to emphasise them because they may be overlooked in the way in which our examples showed.

For these reasons, we shall use an expanded version of the optimising strategy, which reminds us at Stage 3(a) of the need to think about autonomy and justice. We also need a reminder at Stage 2 not to rule out options uncritically on the basis of values which we have never thought to question. Our expanded model, which we call the ethical decision strategy, is given below.

Ethical decision strategy

1 Consider why a decision is necessary (is it necessary?).
2 List the options (i.e. the various possible courses of action). Think about whether any options have been ruled out on ethical grounds. If so, is this justified?
3 For each option:
   (a) list the consequences;

   make sure that implications for autonomy and justice have been included

   (b) consider how likely are any consequences identified under 3(a) (take account of evidence and assess its reliability)
   (c) consider how important the consequences are
   (d) decide whether each of the listed consequences counts for or against the option.
4 Judge between the options in the light of your comments under 3(a)–(d)

Although we have called this the ethical decision strategy, it could be used for any decision. Indeed, the reminders which it incorporates about ethical concepts could be important in many contexts, since we can be faced with decisions whose ethical nature may not be apparent at the outset. We are not claiming that this is the only useful decision making model. In some contexts, it may be appropriate to start with a more specific set of obligations which individuals have in virtue of their position – for example, health workers may have specific obligations to their patients which have not been listed on our model. However, the model presented here can be used in all contexts.

Applying the ethical decision strategy

We now wish to show how the strategy can be used by working systematically through the following two examples.

Example 3: Wedding worries

Jess is about to get married, and her future husband Jim will be out of the country until about a week before the wedding. Two months before the wedding, her future mother-in-law Alice is told that she should have an operation for a relatively serious medical condition, and it would be best to have the operation as soon as possible. The possibility of postponing the wedding is discussed, but Alice does not want this to happen, and chooses to wait until after the wedding to have the operation. Because she thinks Jim will be upset if he knows about her condition, and may even decide to postpone the wedding, she suggests that no-one tells him about the operation until after the wedding. Jess tells Alice that she thinks Jim should be told, but Alice insists that it is better not to tell him. Jess has to decide whether to comply with Alice's suggestion.

We set out below Jess' reasoning process, based on the ethical decision strategy.

1 *Why is a decision necessary?*
I understand why Alice wants Jim not to be told, and I would like to please her, but I am not comfortable about pretending to Jim that everything is normal.

2 *What are the options?*
There are two clear options here:
(i) I tell Jim now about Alice's medical condition.
(ii) I do as Alice wishes, and say nothing to Jim about Alice's medical condition.

3 *Consequences; their likelihood; their importance; pro or con*
Before I list the consequences, I note that I cannot think of any issues relating to justice in making this decision, although there are issues relating to autonomy, as shown below.
Option (i)
Consequence 1 Jim may decide to postpone the wedding, in order that Alice can have the operation earlier. I do not know how likely this is – it may depend upon information about his mother's condition. This consequence is fairly important, since we would all like the wedding to go ahead, and there will be some expense and inconvenience if it is postponed. **Against option (i).**
Consequence 2 Jim's autonomy will certainly be respected, in the sense that he will have an opportunity to make the decision about postponement for himself. It is important that Jim should have the opportunity to exercise an autonomous choice. **For option (i).**
Consequence 3 It is quite likely that Alice will be unhappy that her wishes have not been respected. It is quite important not to upset Alice, especially since she is ill. **Against option (i).**
Consequence 4 Jim will certainly be upset to hear of his mother's ill health, but this is not so important, since he will have to know about it eventually anyway. **Against option (i).**

Option (ii)

Consequence 1   It is certain that the wedding will go ahead as planned, which is important to all of us, but it would not be a disaster if it were postponed until after Alice's recovery. **For option (ii).**

Consequence 2   Alice may suffer discomfort until she has the operation, and her condition may deteriorate. Without more information, I do not know how likely this is. She is my only source of information, and she may be playing down the severity of her condition. Her health is very important. **Against option (ii).**

Consequence 3   Jim's autonomy will have been by-passed, in the sense that he will certainly not have been given the opportunity to make a decision which may affect his mother's health. His autonomy is very important. **Against option (ii).**

Consequence 4   Jim may be annoyed with me and feel that I have let him down. He is not likely to be very angry, but he is likely to think that I should not keep information from him. This consequence is very important, not so much because I will be upset if he is angry, but because his reason for being angry – that I would have failed in my responsibility to be open and honest with him – seems to me to be a good reason. **Against option (ii).**

Consequence 5   Alice will certainly be pleased that I have complied with her suggestion. It is important that she is happy, but I have not promised her that I shall not tell Jim. **For option (ii).**

4   *Judging between the options*

I have identified four consequences of option (i), three of which count against it, and five consequences of option (ii), three of which count against it.

I shall consider how strong are these reasons against each option.

The reasons against option (i) concern consequences which may not occur (i.e. postponement of the wedding), or which will eventually happen even if the option is not acted upon (i.e. Jim's distress about his mother's illness), or which can perhaps be compensated for (Alice may be less upset if I explain my reasoning, and give her support in her illness).

The reasons against option (ii) seem more weighty, since they involve risks to Alice's health, not giving Jim the opportunity to make his own decision, and not fulfilling an obligation, which I believe I have, to be completely honest with my future spouse.

Now I shall assess the reasons for the options.

There is a very strong reason for option (i) – that Jim's autonomy will be respected. I now see that I could have identified another implica-

tion of option (i) – that it would involve failing in an implied obligation, as I have just pointed out. This is another strong reason for telling
Jim.

The reasons for option (ii) are less compelling, since it would be
possible to postpone the wedding without letting anyone down badly,
and since any obligation I have to make Alice happy does not require
that I should do everything she wants me to, and could perhaps be met in
some other way than by not telling Jim what is happening.

The choice now seems clear – that I should act upon option (i) and tell
Jim now about Alice's medical condition.

Example 4: Vegetarianism

Saul's doctor has told him that he has a very high cholesterol level which puts him
at risk of a heart attack. She points out that diet has a great impact on cholesterol
levels, and that if he were to cut out red meat and dairy products from his diet, he
could probably reduce his level considerably. He has read that increasing one's
intake of fruit and vegetables can lower cholesterol levels, and may also reduce
the risk of cancer, and he wonders whether it would be a good idea to switch to a
vegetarian diet.

This is how Saul may reason about the decision.

1 *Why is a decision necessary?*
   I am concerned about my health, and I think that a vegetarian diet may
   be more healthy.

2 *What options are there?*
   (i) Cut red meat and dairy products out of my diet.
   (ii) Cut out all meats and dairy products.
   (iii) Cut out dairy products and adopt a vegetarian diet – no meat, no
   fish.
   (iv) Continue with my present diet, which includes all meats, fish and
   dairy products.

3 *Consequences; their likelihood; their importance; pro or con*
   I have to think about issues concerning autonomy and justice, and my
   first thought was that since this decision concerns only my own health,
   no-one else is going to be affected by it. Then I realised that of course
   those close to me want me to be healthy, so, for their sake as well as for
   my own, I should choose the option which would have the most
   favourable impact on my health. However, that isn't really a matter of

respecting their autonomy or treating them justly – it is more concerned with not harming them. So perhaps there are no implications for autonomy and justice, but I may be able to see that more clearly when I have listed the consequences. I don't need to include enjoyment of food in the consequences, since I like most foods, and think that I would easily adjust to a change of diet.

Option (i)   Cut red meat and dairy products out of my diet.
Consequence 1   Since this is what the doctor recommended, it is likely that this will reduce my cholesterol level, which is very important. **For option (i)**.
Consequence 2   There will be a minor impact on sales of red meat and dairy products, but this is not particularly important, since it is not going to lead to anyone going out of business. **Neither for nor against option (i)**.

Option (ii)   Cut out all meats and dairy products.
Consequence 1   As with option (i), my cholesterol level is likely to fall. **For option (ii)**.
Consequence 2   There may be additional health benefits, since I shall be eating more vegetables, which are supposed to be good for me. However, it may mean that there is less protein in my diet, so I am unsure about the overall health benefit. **More information needed in order to know whether for or against option (ii)**.
Consequence 3   As with option (i), my eating habits will have little impact on anyone's business. **Neither for nor against option (ii)**.

Option (iii)   Cut out dairy products and adopt a vegetarian diet – no meat, no fish.
Consequence 1   A reduction in my cholesterol level as with options (i) and (ii). **For option (iii)**.
Consequence 2   Excluding fish from my diet may further reduce the amount of protein in my diet, and I have read that eating fish is good for health, but I am not sure about this. **More information needed in order to know whether for or against option (iii)**.
Consequence 3   As with options (i) and (ii), my eating habits will have little impact on anyone's business. **Neither for nor against option (ii)**.

Option (iv)   Continue with my present diet, which includes all meats, fish and dairy products.

Consequence 1 My cholesterol level will remain high, and thus I shall still have a high risk of a heart attack. My health is very important. **Against option (iv).**

4 *Judging between the options*

Until I have more information, I shall not be in a position to judge which of the first three options will be most beneficial to my health, but clearly I should rule out option (iv), because it is putting my health at risk. When I have gathered the necessary information, should I just choose the diet which will be best for my health? Is this the only important issue?

The only other kind of consequence I have identified is the impact of my decision on the market for meat, fish and dairy products, and I have judged that the impact of my decision will be small. However, it occurs to me that if many doctors are giving the same advice as mine, and if many people were to decide to switch to a vegetarian diet, there would be a big impact on the meat trade. The long term consequences could be that fewer animals were slaughtered, then eventually fewer would be bred for the food trade. Would this be a good thing? What effect would it have on the options I've been considering if I thought about them as choices for a whole population, instead of just for one individual?

We often hear that animals bred for food are kept in bad conditions, so if the whole population became vegetarian, some suffering would be eliminated, and that is surely important. But perhaps this suffering could be eliminated by improving the conditions in which animals are kept.

Of course, that would mean that they still have to be slaughtered. Can they be slaughtered painlessly? If so, would this mean that there were no bad consequences of meat-eating? Or is there something wrong with killing animals anyway? After all, we would think it was wrong to kill human beings.

I'm beginning to wonder whether this decision *does* involve issues of autonomy or justice. It seems a bit odd to talk about respecting the autonomy of animals, because we tend to think of animals as not being capable of exercising autonomy – not being able to reflect about options and make choices. But is justice involved – is it unjust to kill animals, when we would not do that to humans? Should we treat humans and animals equally in this respect, because they are equal in some important way?

I now realise that I have to do much more thinking about what my attitude to animals should be, and not simply find out which option is best for my health. I may find that option (ii), which allows me to eat

fish, is best for my health, but I need to consider whether there is something wrong with killing fish.

In the process of trying to make this decision, Saul has discovered that it is
a much more complex matter than he initially thought. What do you think
are the answers to the questions he asks in section 4 above? We shall say
more about the moral status of animals in later chapters.

Not only did Saul's decision process turn out to be more complex than
initially anticipated, but also the reason as to why a decision needed to be
made shifted focus, in such a way that the decision became much more obviously one involving ethical considerations. Thus the example illustrates two
things about decision making in general. First, it reinforces our earlier
comments about the need for a decision making model which reminds us
about ethical issues, even when we are not sure at the outset that an ethical
issue is involved. Second, it shows us that the first question in the decision
making model (Why is a decision necessary?) must not be allowed to dictate
and thereby possibly restrict our reasoning process. Once we start thinking
about consequences, autonomy and justice, we may see that the problem
which first prompted us to reason through the decision is not the only relevant matter. For example, Saul initially thought that a decision was needed
only because of risks to his health. If he had let this dictate his decision, he
would not have considered animal welfare, and would therefore have been
less well equipped to defend whatever decision he did eventually make.

The example also illustrates a feature more specifically of ethical decisions.
Sometimes it is not enough to ask 'What will happen if *I* do this?' The appropriate question may be 'What would happen if *everyone* did this?' In this
example, Saul has not finally made his decision, and we have not said what
that decision should be. But if he were to conclude that the widespread practice of meat-eating was wrong on the grounds that it involved killing animals,
he could not then excuse his own meat-eating by saying 'It will make no
difference to how many animals are killed if *I* give up eating meat'.

It is now time for you to apply the decision making model. As you work
through the following exercise, remember the important points which we
have just identified: during your reasoning process, you may modify your
answer to the question as to why a decision is necessary; even with decisions
which seem merely personal, you should ask 'What would be the consequences if everyone did this?'

Exercise 5 Making decisions

Use the ethical decision strategy in order to make decisions on the following issues. If you find that your decision requires further information which it is difficult for you to get, say what your decision would be if you had reliable information about a particular question. Make a note of any ethical concepts upon which you rely.

1 A friend comes to you in great distress and says that he has a problem which he wants to talk about, but he wants to be sure that you will not mention his problem to anyone else. You promise that his secret will be safe – you will not tell anyone what he tells you. He then reveals that he has just learnt that he is HIV positive. Some months later, a female acquaintance tells you that she is dating your friend, and he later admits to you that she does not know about his HIV status. You must make a decision as to whether to tell her yourself.

2 Imagine that you are a member of parliament in a country in which abortion is illegal. You know that 'back-street' abortions take place, and that they involve risks to the health of the women who undergo them. You also know that many women think they should have the right to have an abortion without breaking the law. You must make a decision as to whether to vote in favour of a law permitting abortion. You must also decide what the law would have to say about time limits (i.e. up to how many weeks of pregnancy would abortion be permissible), and about whether every pregnant woman would be entitled to abortion, or would it be restricted to certain circumstances (e.g. if abortion resulted from rape, or if the foetus had a disability).

3 Read the following passage, which comes from a leading article in the *Independent* newspaper on 2 October 1993.

The criminalisation of cannabis derives from a number of prejudices and misconceptions. Although the drug is not entirely harmless, it is less harmful than tobacco. It is not addictive, nor dangerous in moderate quantities, and it does not provoke violent or anti-social behaviour. It mostly induces nothing worse than a state of rather happy, foolish withdrawal. It was partly this effect that worried orthodox society in the sixties, because it became associated with the demotivation of an entire generation that was exaggeratedly seen as dropping out of the acquisitive, consumerist society. Cannabis was felt to be subversive.

Since then, successive generations have responded normally to economic stimuli and remained as acquisitive as anyone could wish. But they have continued to take cannabis. Almost all 25-year-olds in London have tried it, according to a recent survey by *Time Out* magazine. Cannabis should therefore have lost its association with drop-outs and have come to be seen as a recreational drug, offering much the same sort of respite from reality as alcohol but with less dangerous side-effects. It is also being found to have a widening variety of valuable medicinal qualities, particularly for the alleviation of multiple sclerosis.

In a period of rising crime, when practically every householder and car-owner feels vulnerable, and when peaceful citizens form vigilante groups because they are insufficiently protected by the proper authorities, it is absurd that the police and the courts should have had to spend valuable time dealing with 47,616 drug offences in 1991, and probably more last year, of which about 85 per cent concerned cannabis. Legalising the drug would save substantial amounts of time and money as well as bringing in tax revenue from legal sales. It would reduce the number of crimes committed to raise money for cannabis by lowering the price, unless heavily taxed, and undermine the power of the criminal underworld.

Make a decision as to whether the use of cannabis should be legalised.

4 Read the following passage from an article in the *Independent on Sunday*, 21 January 1996.
Annie Lindsell is living on borrowed time. She suffers from the terminal illness motor neurone disease and is enduring a long deterioration into death.

Week by week, her life changes for the worse. She can no longer go to the bathroom alone, or dress herself or wash. She notices she can no longer grip a cup as she once did. She fears eating out will soon become too embarrassing to contemplate. 'I end up wearing more food than eating it', she says. It is the lack of dignity she hates most.

She is brave and determined but knows that, barring a miracle cure, her prognosis is not good. Most sufferers survive just three years from diagnosis. She has already lasted four. But when the time comes, she wants to die quickly.

Next week she will appear at the House of Commons to explain why she believes there should be a change in the law so that she can die at a time and in a manner she chooses.

Make a decision as to whether there should be a change in the law so that it will no longer be illegal for doctors to bring about the deaths of patients like Annie Lindsell. If you decide that euthanasia should be made legal, be specific about the kinds of cases to which it should apply.

5 Read the following passage.

A river tumbles through forested ravines and rocky gorges towards the sea. The state hydro-electricity commission sees the falling water as untapped energy. Building a dam across one of the gorges would provide three years of employment for a thousand people, and longer term employment for twenty or thirty. The dam would store enough water to ensure that the state could economically meet its energy needs for the next decade. This would encourage the establishment of energy-intensive industry thus further contributing to employment and economic growth.

The rough terrain of the river valley makes it accessible only to the reasonably fit, but it is nevertheless a favoured spot for bush-walking. The river itself attracts the more daring whitewater rafters. Deep in the sheltered valleys are stands of rare Huon Pine, many of the trees being over a thousand years old. The valleys and gorges are home to many birds and animals, including an endangered species of marsupial mouse that has seldom been found outside the valley. There may be other rare plants and animals as well, but no-one knows, for scientists are yet to investigate the region fully.

(P. Singer, *Practical Ethics*, Cambridge University Press, 1993, p. 264)

Make a decision as to whether the dam should be built.

Chapter 5

Concepts in practical ethics

In earlier chapters we have said that a concept is an idea or a set of ideas associated with a particular word or phrase, and that at least one ethical concept – harm – is basic to the whole enterprise of moral reasoning, in that you could not be said to be engaged in moral reasoning at all if you took no account of it. We have also suggested that two other concepts – autonomy and justice – play a crucial role in reasoning well about moral issues. Other concepts which are relevant to many ethical issues have come up in examples and in passages of reasoning for the exercises which you worked on in Chapters 2 and 3. When you made decisions on the topics in Exercise 5 in the last chapter, you may have relied on moral concepts which we have not yet discussed.

We provided brief definitions of autonomy and justice, but not of harm, since we have assumed that we all have some idea as to what is meant by harm. However, each of these concepts could be analysed in greater detail, and this may be something which you will feel able to do when you have read this chapter. Many other concepts are used in ethical discussions, for example, cruelty, bravery, and honesty.

In Chapter 2 we pointed out that you may need to clarify to your own satisfaction the meanings of words or phrases which you find in other people's reasoning. This is not the only context in which clarification may be necessary, since others may ask *you* to clarify what *you* mean by certain words. It is important that we have an understanding of the meaning of the terms (i.e. words or phrases) which we use in reasoning about ethical issues, and some of these terms will be the words used to refer to concepts. It will be useful to approach the clarification of concepts by thinking first about how we would clarify terms in general.

Clarifying terms

Definitions

When we come across an unfamiliar word in someone else's writing, the obvious thing to do is to look it up in a dictionary, where we will find a definition, often in the form of a synonym (if you don't know what 'synonym' means, look it up in a dictionary!). For example, if you were to read a famous speech on capital punishment made in Parliament in 1868 by John Stuart Mill, you would find him considering whether the time had come to 'abrogate' the death penalty. 'Abrogate' is not a word which we often use in everyday speech, so you might look it up, and find it defined as 'repeal' or 'cancel'. Not all words are easily defined by one single other word. Suppose you were told that John Stuart Mill was an advocate of 'utilitarianism', and you wanted to know what that meant. A dictionary definition may tell you that 'utilitarianism' is 'a doctrine that actions are justified if they are useful or for the benefit of the majority'.

Our principal aim in this chapter is to help you to focus on your own understanding of the moral concepts which *you* use when making ethical decisions. You need to be able to clarify to your own satisfaction – and in such a way that you would be able to communicate this to others – the meanings of the terms upon which you rely. If you were asked to clarify some single words in common usage, it would not be at all difficult to give a definition. Suppose you are asked what the word 'sister' means. You know what has to be true of someone who is a sister, so you would probably give the definition 'female sibling'. This is a definition which gives the necessary and sufficient conditions for the application of the term – being female and being a sibling are each necessary conditions for being a sister, and taken together they are sufficient conditions for being a sister.

There are two minor problems with this definition. First, it gives the necessary and sufficient conditions for being a sister in only one sense of the term. Since nuns and some nurses can also be referred to as 'sisters', it is possible to be a sister in these senses without having any siblings. This illustrates the fact that whether or not an adequate definition has been given can depend upon the context in which the word is being used. The other problem is that the definition will clarify the term only for those who already know, for example, what 'sibling' means. This term could, of course, be defined in its turn, but since this definition would use other words, it is clear that giving definitions assumes that those with whom one is communicating must understand some terms. This was illustrated also by the definition of 'abrogate' above, which required understanding of the meaning of either 'repeal' or 'cancel'. Thus when you wish to clarify the terms you use in such a way that others will understand your meaning, you need to have some idea of the level of competence in language of your audience, or you need to express yourself in the simplest possible terms, so that the widest possible audience would be capable of understanding.

Not all words can easily be defined by producing a set of necessary and sufficient conditions. This can be true even of words which are in very common use. In Exercise 4 the passage by Mary Midgley about boxing begins by asking 'Is boxing still a sport?' How could we answer this question without having some idea as to how 'sport' must be defined? (In fact, Midgley does not define it, but she makes it clear that she believes that any activity which involves physical injury to the human head is 'not a reasonable sporting activity'. This tells us what she thinks is ruled out of the category of 'sport'.) Try for yourself to define 'sport', before you read any further. You will probably find that when you think you have produced a neat definition which gives necessary and sufficient conditions, you then wonder whether some activity which lacks one of these conditions should nevertheless be regarded as a sport. For example, suppose your definition was 'a competitive activity involving physical exercise', you might then wonder whether snooker, which doesn't involve very strenuous physical exercise, is a sport, or whether rock climbing, which isn't a competitive activity, is a sport. By thinking of examples of particular sports, you may be able to come up with a list of characteristics which are typical of sports, without it being necessary for an activity to have all of those characteristics in order to be a sport. This example draws our attention to the way in which thinking of examples can help to clarify meanings.

Sport: A physical activity which people participate in as a game, hobby, or career.

Clarification using examples

In Chapter 2, we sought to evaluate the principle that treatment of self-inflicted illness should be given a lower priority than treatment for those who have taken care of their health. In order to do this we need to clarify what is meant by 'self-inflicted illness'.

Our initial strategy could be to list what we take to be examples of self-inflicted illness, (e.g. lung cancer caused by smoking, heart disease caused by an excessively fatty diet) then identify what these examples have in common

Self-inflicted illness: An illness or disease caused by willingfully excessive amounts of a substance within a persons daily life.

111

in order to produce a definition. Or we could aim to come up with an initial definition (e.g. 'an illness caused by the actions or behaviour of the person who is ill'), then think of the implications of this definition – i.e. what kinds of illness does this include? Whichever of these two we choose, we shall find that the particular examples play a role in clarifying the definition, because once we see the implications of our initial definition, we may see that we have not defined the term sufficiently tightly. We pointed out in Chapter 2 that the simple definition above would mean that we had to include as self-inflicted any illness caused by one's own actions, even if the individual involved had no idea that the actions could cause the illness. This seems unreasonable, if every self-inflicted illness were to be given lower priority for treatment, since it would mean that individuals were penalised for their lack of knowledge.

This last point illustrates an important aspect of clarifying concepts – that the purpose for which the concept is to be used may make a difference to the definition upon which we settle. The purpose of using the term 'self-inflicted illness' in this context is to identify people who should be given a lower priority for medical treatment. If we were sure that this should not apply to people who did not know that their behaviour would make them ill, or to people who could not help acting as they did – e.g. drug addicts – then we would want our definition to exclude these cases, and might revise it to read 'an illness which has knowingly been caused by the deliberate and free action of an individual'.

Clarifying concepts

We are now ready to think about clarifying some of the concepts we have encountered in arguments and decisions about ethical issues. Let us just refresh our memory as to what we mean by the word 'concept' – a concept is an idea or a set of ideas associated with a particular word or phrase. Before we work through an example of clarification, here is a short exercise in understanding the way in which others are using particular concepts.

Exercise 6 Identifying concepts

For each of the following passages, identify the crucial concept used, and express in your own words what the author's definition of the concept is. Think about whether this is an appropriate definition.

1 First we really must clear our heads on the question of rights. Animals have none. Rights only apply to human beings, because rights are indissolubly linked to responsibilities. Rights spring from human agreements, social contracts among fellow citizens. Rights come linked to moral obligations. That doesn't mean we should condone cruelty or gratuitous pain. We think badly of a man who wilfully steps on a butterfly, but that doesn't confer rights on the butterfly.

(Polly Toynbee, *Independent*, 25 January 1995)

Rights—applicable only to humans, responsibilities linked to moral obligations

2 The following is an extract from the final chapter in John Harris's book *The Value of Life*, in which he envisages the possibility of people having themselves frozen whilst close to death yet still alive, in the hope of resuscitation at some time in the future when a cure for their illness would have been discovered. It is this frozen state to which he is referring when he talks about 'suspended animation' and 'the frozen un-dead'.

what is the concept here?

If, for example, it ceased to be plausible to attribute to individuals the possession of capacities that had been dormant or inactive for some time and if this proved to be the case with the capacity for wishing to continue to exist, then the status of those in suspended animation would dramatically and significantly change. It might, for example, then be clear that after reasonably long periods in suspended anima-tion individuals moved from the class of people who possess self-consciousness but who merely cannot at the moment exercise it, to the class of potential people who do not possess self-consciousness but who might re-acquire it, who have the potential for it.

If this were a reasonable interpretation of their state then, like the foetus and the neonate, the frozen un-dead would not have to be protected in quite the same way as are persons. There are two difficul-ties here. The first is that of resolving whether or not it is right to say that the frozen still retain a capacity for wishing to live. The second problem is whether or not we can be sufficiently confident of our answer to the first question to allow so much to turn on it. It may after all be a matter of life or death for those involved.

3 In this extract from Peter Singer's book *Animal Liberation*, the sentence giving the author's definition of the crucial term has been omitted.

The taking into account of the interests of the being, whatever those interests may be, must according to the principle of equality, be extended to all beings, black or white, masculine or feminine, human or nonhuman.It is on this basis that the case against racism an d the case against sexism must ultimately rest; and it is in accordance with this principle that the attitude that we may call 'speciesism', by analogy with racism, must also be condemned.If. possessing a higher degr ee of intelligence does not entitle one human to use another for his own ends, how can it entitle humans to exploit nonhumans for the same purpose?.As long as we remember that we should give the same respect to the lives of animals as we give to the lives of those humans at a similar mental level, we shall not go far wrong.

An example – clarifying the concept of rights

One of the concepts which has come up frequently in our examples of reasoning is the concept of rights. We shall use this as an example to illustrate how concepts can be clarified. First let us summarise, as a series of steps, the important aspects of clarification which we identified in the discussion of the meaning of 'self-inflicted illness'.

Summary *Steps to clarify concepts*

1 If possible, think of a typical instance, or a number of examples of the term which needs to be clarified.
2 Write out an initial definition. (At this stage, you could use a dictionary definition, or you could use your examples in order to come up with a general definition.)
3 Think about whether the terms of this definition need to be further analysed. You are going to have to answer questions about what the definition implies you should *do*. If the initial definition is too vague and general for you to answer such questions, try to make it more specific by further clarifying the terms used in the definition.
4 Consider what your initial definition implies:

(a) are there other cases to which the term must apply?

(b) in view of the *purpose* of using the term, what does it tell us we should do in relation to particular examples?

5 Consider whether, in the light of your answers to 4 (a) and (b), your definition needs to be modified.

It can be fruitful to go through these steps in discussion with others. For example, you may come up with your own initial definition, then compare this with others in the group, and tell each other which terms in the definition need to be further analysed. You could try this with the concept of rights before you read our analysis below. As with our analysis of arguments in Chapter 3, this provides an example of the kind of analysis which practice will help you to work towards.

1 What examples of rights can we think of, in particular in relation to the arguments and decisions we have discussed so far? In Chapter 1, the argument talked about the rights of human beings and of the unborn child; in Exercise 6, the article by Polly Toynbee argued against the possibility of animal rights. So we could say that human rights, animal rights and the rights of embryos and foetuses are all examples of rights.

We can also think of examples of rights in a different way – not just examples of the sorts of entities which may have rights, but examples of the kinds of rights which these entities may be claimed to have. We have seen claims that we have rights to equal treatment before the law (in Edwina Currie's article about the age of consent for homosexuals), that human beings and foetuses have a right to life (p.35), that animals may have rights (in the extract from Jonathon Porritt in Exercise 3).

What these examples of rights have in common is that they all imply that certain entities should be protected in some way.

2 We could state our first definition as follows:

> 'Rights' are entitlements to be treated in certain ways, or to have one's interests taken into account.

3 This definition gives us a starting point for clarification, but it is still too vague to tell us anything about how we should act. For example, what kinds of entitlements are we talking about? Do we mean legal entitlements? Well certainly there are such things as legal entitlements – for

[handwritten margin note: Break down the words further]

example, in democratic societies most adults are legally entitled to vote – but if we inserted the word 'legal' into our definition this would narrow its scope. We wouldn't be able to claim that people have a right to treatment which is denied them by the laws of the country in which they live. Organisations such as Amnesty International publicise the plight of people being held in detention and, in some cases, cruelly treated, for expressing views which are unacceptable to certain governments. We could say that these people have a right to express dissent without being punished, even if their country's laws do not give them a legal right to free speech. Such a claim assumes that moral rights are universal, rather than dependent upon a particular political system, as legal rights are. So we could modify the definition to read:

> 'Rights' are universal moral entitlements to be treated in certain ways, or to have one's interests taken into account.

This definition suggests a relationship between the concept of rights and the concept of justice, if justice is to be defined as 'treating equals equally'. If everyone has an entitlement to be treated in a certain way, then it would be unjust to fail to treat some people in that way. However, the concept of rights imposes stronger moral demands than merely treating people equally. It aims to tell us how people should be treated.

4 Can we now think about the implications of this definition in order to clarify it further, first by thinking about cases to which the term applies?
(a) The definition is still somewhat vague, because we haven't specified in which ways people, animals and foetuses are entitled to be treated. Let us take one example – that of the right to life, and ask, what does it imply to say that one has such a right? It must mean that anyone who wants to go on living should not be prevented from doing so. If everyone has a right to life then no-one ought to kill anyone else against their will. In J.J. Thomson's story about the violinist (Exercise 4), another issue about the right to life emerged. Did the violinist have the right to use someone else's kidneys in order to stay alive? This is, of course, a far-fetched example, but the question it raises is whether there are circumstances in which the right to life requires not just that other people refrain from killing you, but that they take some positive action to keep you alive. And this issue is relevant to, for example, cases of people with heart disease who may or may not be resuscitated by doctors after a heart attack.

Remember that we are trying to clarify our definition, rather than aiming to settle the question as to exactly what the right to life involves.

What the example shows us about the claim that someone has a particular right is that such a claim may imply that everyone else has a duty to refrain from certain actions (in the case of the right to life, to refrain from killing), or it may imply that at least someone else has a duty to act positively in some way (in the case of the right to life, to take action to prolong life), or it may imply both of these.

Because of these two possible interpretations, some writers have produced separate definitions for these two categories, calling them negative rights and positive rights. Negative rights are rights to other people's forbearance, so if you have a negative right, everyone else has a duty to refrain from certain actions – for example, if you have a right not to be operated on without your consent, then everyone must refrain from operating on you if you have not consented. Positive rights are rights to have other people act positively in some way, so if you have a positive right then someone else has a duty to do something – for example, if we have a right to a certain standard of health care, then someone has a duty to provide the appropriate health care.

{ Negative rights

{ Positive rights

The idea of negative rights makes it very clear who has certain duties – everyone does. The idea of positive rights may be harder to accept, because it implies that at least someone has a duty to act, but does not specify precisely who has the duty.

There is another way in which the definition is still a little vague. What is meant to be the scope of the word 'universal'? We introduced it as a result of reflection on the universality of *human* rights, but it could be interpreted as applying more widely to include animals also.

(b)   Let us think explicitly about the purpose of using the term 'rights'. Typically, when people claim that they have a right, they are aiming to remind other people of certain moral obligations owed to them. Indeed, the definitions of negative and positive rights emphasise that others have duties. This prompts two questions which may further clarify the concept.

(i)   Are the obligations imposed by rights meant to override all other moral considerations?

There are two ways of thinking about this question, which we can illuminate by using the example of the right to life. First, if there is such a thing as a right to life, are there no *exceptions* to it, i.e. are there no circumstances in which one person is morally entitled to kill another? We generally regard killing in self-defence, where you kill an attacker who would otherwise have killed you, as morally justified. This suggests that even if there is such a thing as a right to life, individuals can forfeit that right by their own wrong actions.

(ii) Is the language of 'rights' simply a way of speaking about moral obligations?

This question forces us to think about whether rights can possibly be real entities out there in the world, or when we say that there exists a right to life, is this just another way of saying that in most circumstances killing is wrong? Do we really need the concept of rights in order to be able to say everything we need to say about morality?

5 The final stage is to review the definition we offered at stage 3, and think about whether it needs to be modified.

We are going to leave this exercise for you to sort out to your own satisfaction, but we shall summarise the extent to which we have clarified the term 'rights'.

Nothing we have said in sections 4 (a) and 4 (b) (i) implies that the original definition is radically mistaken, but it is not sufficiently detailed in the following respects:

It does not make clear whether rights are absolute moral demands which allow no exceptions, and cannot be overridden in any circumstances.

It does not make clear whether there can be such things as positive rights, requiring not just refraining from actions which would interfere with others' moral entitlements, but also positive actions to uphold those entitlements.

It does not make clear the scope of the term 'universal'. Are rights possessed only by humans, or by animals also? This prompts the question as to what characteristics an entity would have to have in order to possess rights.

The questions raised in section 4 (b) (ii) may have convinced you that moral rights are not real entities. If so, you may wish to begin your clarification of the concept as follows:

> The concept of rights does not imply that moral rights really exist, but it is used in order to emphasise certain very important moral obligations.

You would then need to go on to specify whether these obligations are absolute; whether they merely require us to abstain from interference with others' lives, or require positive action; and to which entities these obligations are owed.

If you think that moral rights are real entities, you may wish to ask yourself some further questions – in particular as to how you could justify the claim that rights really exist. Such a question goes deep into philosophical territory, and you may be able to settle moral dilemmas without exploring it. However, you may be interested in the moral theories underlying the idea of rights. In the next chapter, we shall make brief comments about the connection between rights and two moral theories – utilitarianism and Kant's moral theory. The kind of theory most closely associated with the concept of rights is known as contract theory.

Contract theories encompass the conception of rights expressed in the extract from Polly Toynbee's article presented in Exercise 6, where she says, 'Rights spring from human agreements, social contracts among fellow citizens'. The idea of a social contract (proposed most famously by Locke, Hobbes and Rousseau) is the idea of an agreement between individuals, or between individuals and the governing power, to surrender some liberty in return for the advantages of living in a well-ordered society. So it is first and foremost a concept in political philosophy, explaining the origins and basis of political systems. If it is applicable to rights, it is most obviously applicable to legal rights. But the idea of a social contract is also sometimes used as an explanation of how we come to have a moral system. So to justify the idea of moral rights by referring to a social contract would be to say that moral rights are defined by what we agree upon as members of a social group.

But if different social groups can agree on different sets of rights, and if rights are determined by what societies as a matter of fact agree on, then we don't seem to be talking about universal rights at all. If moral rights are universal, then all societies *should* respect them, even if the members of those societies have agreed not to do so. Consider whether this idea of a social contract means that we are discovering rights, or inventing them. If we are inventing them, then they are not necessarily universal. If we are discovering them, then the idea of social agreement cannot be sufficient as a basis for rights. It would be possible for societies to reach agreement, and yet be wrong. So we cannot fully explain the origin and basis of moral rights by referring to what societies *as a matter of fact* agree upon.

Some social contract theorists suggest that moral rights are determined not by what we actually agree upon but by what *rational beings would* agree on. John Rawls put forward a theory of social justice which implies that rights are those claims to entitlement which rational beings would agree should be respected – on condition that these rational beings did not know what position (in terms of power, wealth, etc.) they themselves were going to occupy in a society, and did not know what their own talents and abilities would be. Imagine that the only thing you know about yourself is that you are a human being – then consider what rights you would want the society you live in to respect.

This puts a lot of weight on the idea of rationality. But surely our rationality would need something to work on – some understanding as to what is in the interests of human beings. You couldn't just rely on knowing what you want, because you are not supposed to know anything about yourself, except that you are a human being. You would have to have good reasons for thinking that human beings should have certain rights, perhaps based on some ideas about basic human needs which any society should seek to meet.

This conception of moral rights as based on agreement makes it difficult to see how rights could be extended to animals, since animals would not be able to enter into agreements with humans. This is why Polly Toynbee insists that animals cannot have rights.

Another example – the concept of a person

The extract from J.J. Thomson's article on abortion in Exercise 4, and the passage from John Harris in Exercise 6 refer to the concept of a person, a concept which is often claimed to be relevant to some practical ethical issues. Using our model for clarification of concepts, let us think about how we should define 'person'.

1 It seems strange to start by thinking of examples of persons, since we would probably end up listing all our acquaintances, but we could instead think of a typical instance of a person, namely an adult human being.

2 The initial definition suggested by this is the same as we would find in most dictionaries, i.e.:

> A person is an individual human being.

3 There is nothing vague or mysterious about this definition – indeed it seems so clear and so obviously correct that we may wonder why we need to try to clarify the term at all.

4 (a) To which other cases does 'person' apply?
We said initially that a typical instance of a person was an adult human being. Our definition is 'an individual human being'. This includes children, of course, at any age. Perhaps it also includes foetuses, since even though they are dependent on another individual, they exist as individuals in the sense of having their own genetic identity, and they belong to the human species. It excludes animals, and it excludes beings which may have evolved on other planets. So far, you may be happy with the definition and its implications.
(b) What is the purpose of using the term, and what are the implications of this purpose for particular examples?
Although the term 'rights' is very commonly used in discussions of ethical issues, the term 'person' is more often used in ethical contexts by philosophers than by members of the general public. So we should

examine why philosophers are using this term. In the extract from J.J. Thomson, the author aims to convince us that there are circumstances in which abortion is permissible even if the foetus is a person. Those who hold what Thomson calls 'the extreme view' insist that the foetus is a person. This is because *if* the foetus is a person, the idea that it has a right to life, or that it would be wrong to kill it, seems to gain support. For the purpose of her argument, Thomson doesn't need to define 'person', because she doesn't rest her case on a claim that the foetus is not a person.

John Harris, however, *is* concerned with defining 'person', and his purpose in using the concept is to sort out our moral obligations to different entities. Persons have more value, according to Harris, than non-persons, and if such a claim is to be of practical use, we must be able to point to characteristics which determine whether or not an entity is a person. In the extract by Harris in Exercise 6, in which he is discussing what our moral obligations might be towards the 'frozen un-dead', two characteristics of persons are mentioned 'self-consciousness' and 'the capacity for wishing to continue to exist'. If we define person in the way Harris does, then we shall probably conclude that embryos and foetuses are not persons, because it is difficult to accept that at such an early stage of development a human being could be conscious of itself and wish to continue to exist. On the other hand, since Harris does not say that being 'human' is a necessary characteristic for being a person, his definition could allow that aliens and perhaps some non-human animals could be persons. They would be persons if they had the capacity to wish to continue to exist.

Harris's analysis of the concept of a person is one which is accepted also by Peter Singer in *Practical Ethics*, and accords with a definition offered by John Locke, who wrote that the term 'person' stands for 'a thinking intelligent being, that has reason and reflection, and can consider itself the same thinking thing, in different times and places'.

5 Given that the purpose of using the concept 'person' in discussions about practical ethical issues is to support the claim that we have different moral obligations to different entities, you may wish to define 'person' in a different way from that which we offered at Stage 2. These are the questions you need to think about:

Are persons more valuable than other entities?

If so, what are the characteristics which make them more valuable? (e.g. is being human sufficient to make an entity more valuable than any others?)

Are characteristics such as 'the capacity for wishing to continue to exist' relevant to questions about how we should treat embryos, foetuses and animals? (Some philosophers think that this capacity *is* relevant, on the grounds that it would, for example, be much more clearly wrong to kill an entity which could value its own potential future life in this way.)

Is it possible to give necessary and sufficient conditions for the application of the term 'person', or is it similar to 'sport' in that there are a number of characteristics of persons, but one doesn't need to possess them all in order to be a person?

Now that we have worked through examples of analysing concepts, you could try some analysis for yourself in Exercise 7.

Exercise 7 Analysing concepts

You will probably find that this exercise is most fruitful if you work with others in a small group.

1 Analyse the concept of 'speciesism', which was introduced by Peter Singer in the third of our passages in Exercise 6. Singer's own definition, which we omitted, was 'Speciesism…. is a prejudice or attitude of bias toward the interests of members of one's own species and against those of other species'.

2 Analyse the concept of harm.

3 Analyse the concept of autonomy.

4 Analyse the concept of honesty.

5 Analyse the concept of obscenity.

1. Various forms of sexually explicit content
2. Def: something that is considered offensive or disgusting by accepted standards or morality and/or decency
3. What are "accepted standards of decency"
4. Ex 1: War crimes to civillians in Ukraine
   Ex 2: Contemporary art

Chapter 6

Moral principles and moral theories

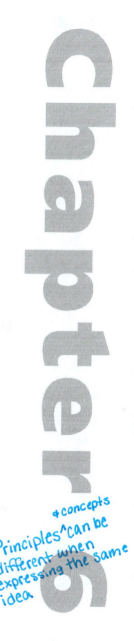

In Chapter 1, we defined a principle as a general rule or recommendation which applies to a number of specific cases. We also observed that principles can be closely related to moral concepts, a point which was reinforced in the last chapter when we considered whether, for example, justifying a moral claim on the basis of the concept of a right to life is just another way of saying that in most circumstances killing is wrong. This illustrates one way in which concepts and principles can be related – that they can be different ways of expressing the same idea. There is another way in which they may be related – perhaps there are some very general moral principles which underlie a number of more specific principles and concepts. 'Killing is wrong' is a moral principle, and thus, in accordance with our definition, it is a general rule which applies to specific cases. But there is a sense in which it is also specific – it tells us about a particular *class* of actions which are wrong, rather than providing a principle of such generality that we can work out from it whether *any* proposed action is wrong. Is there a general principle of this kind?

In this chapter we shall examine two moral theories each of which offers its own distinctive, and supposedly over-arching, moral

[handwritten margin note:] ← Principles & concepts can be different when expressing the same idea

principle. These are not the only moral theories which philosophers have put forward, but we concentrate on them because the principles they offer are clearly addressed to individuals, and intended as a basis for decisions as to what is the right thing to do in any particular situation. This chapter thus gives some insight into moral theory and also the opportunity to practise the skill of applying principles to specific cases. You may wish to increase your knowledge of moral theory by studying two other important theories – the social contract idea of John Rawls (J. Rawls, *A Theory of Justice*, Cambridge: Harvard University Press, 1971), which was mentioned in Chapter 5 in relation to the concept of rights, and the idea of 'virtue ethics', dating from Aristotle, which emphasises the importance of good character, and which is briefly discussed in James Rachels' *The Elements of Moral Philosophy*, McGraw-Hill, 1993. We shall not cover these theories in detail because 'virtue ethics' does not offer a single clear principle, and although Rawls theory includes principles of justice, these are intended as a basis for social organisation rather than a basis for individuals to make their ethical decisions.

In Chapter 2 we suggested the following strategy for assessing principles: think about some of the cases to which the principle must apply; consider whether any of these applications shows that there is something wrong with the principle; think about the way in which the principle should be modified. We shall take a practical approach of this kind in order to evaluate the two moral theories. We shall also consider the relationship of each theory to the moral concepts we have discussed – in particular to the concepts of harm, justice and autonomy, which we have suggested are crucial to reasoning well about practical ethical issues.

We shall not discuss the way in which each of these theories seeks to *justify* its major principle. If you want this kind of detail about the theories, you can read J.S. Mill's *Utilitarianism* (1863) and H.J. Paton's *The Moral Law: Kant's Groundwork of the Metaphysic of Morals* (1948). For our purposes, it is sufficient to note that the principles proposed by these theories have some plausibility, and help to illuminate discussions in practical ethics.

Utilitarianism

The moral theory of utilitarianism originated with Jeremy Bentham in the late eighteenth century, and was advocated by John Stuart Mill in the nineteenth century, but this does not mean that it is out-dated and of merely historical interest. Many present-day philosophers apply the framework of utilitarianism to practical ethical issues such as abortion, euthanasia, war and so on.

Clarifying the principle

The crucial feature of utilitarianism is its insistence that the rightness or wrongness of an action is determined by its consequences for everyone affected by it – the theory is described as a consequentialist theory. The early utilitarians claimed that the best consequences would be those which contained the greatest amount of happiness. John Stuart Mill's statement of the utilitarian principle was: 'Utility, or the Greatest Happiness Principle, holds that actions are right in proportion as they tend to promote happiness, wrong as they tend to produce the reverse of happiness' (J.S. Mill, *Utilitarianism*, 1863 – Chapter 2).

Modern utilitarians, instead of talking about 'happiness', are likely to say that what we should aim for is the maximum satisfaction of interests or of preferences. Peter Singer, for example, suggests that we should 'adopt the course of action most likely to maximise the interests of those affected' (Singer 1993: 13), and also that we should judge actions 'by the extent to which they accord with the preferences of any beings affected by the action or its consequences' (Singer 1993: 94).

The definitions raise a number of questions. First, is it the *actual* consequences (as Mill's definition suggests), or the *expected* consequences (which Singer implies) which determine the rightness of an action? If utilitarianism is to be a practical guide to conduct, then since we cannot in advance know the actual consequences of actions, it is most sensible to regard the principle as referring to expected consequences. Second, should we be judging what *a particular action* is likely to bring about (as Singer suggests) or should we (as Mill seems to think) judge whether *actions of this kind* generally bring about the best consequences? We shall return to this question later in this chapter when we discuss act-utilitarianism and rule-utilitarianism.

The definitions also illustrate a problem which arises from the classical version of the theory as expressed by John Stuart Mill, which tells us to maximise happiness. The problem is that it is not clear whether we should aim to give people what *we* think will make them happy – i.e. to give them what is judged to be in their interests – or to give them what *they* say will make them happy – i.e. to satisfy their expressed preferences. In 1994 in the Netherlands, where euthanasia is tolerated for terminally ill patients, a doctor was prosecuted for administering a lethal drug to a woman who was severely depressed after the deaths of her two sons and said she no longer wanted to live. The doctor acted to satisfy her preference, but this may not have been in her interests if she could have been helped through her depression. However, Peter Singer clearly thinks that, in general, consideration of interests and consideration of preferences will produce the same result, since he talks about: 'the plausible move of taking a person's interests to be what, on

Handwritten margin notes:
- Def of Utilitarianism
- Best consequences → greatest amount of happiness
- Right actions → promote happiness
- Wrong actions → discourage happiness

balance and after reflection on all the relevant facts, a person prefers' (Singer 1993: 94).

Let us assume that we can generally safely judge interests on the basis of preferences, and think about how we would apply the utilitarian principle 'Act so as to produce maximum satisfaction of preferences of those affected by an action'. Is it now clear what we have to do? Obviously we have to think about how our actions will affect others as well as ourselves, and what those others will prefer. But who or what counts as 'others'? Presumably we must take into account anyone or anything capable of having preferences. So if animals have preferences, even if plants have preferences, we must take those preferences into account.

Applying the utilitarian principle

First, try for yourself to apply the utilitarian principle to the following examples. In each case, work out what the principle tells you is the right thing to do, and consider whether this shows that there is something wrong with the principle.

Complications for Utilitarians

1. Non-egoistic

2. Do these consequences refer to actual consequences or expected consequences?

3. Does this theory refer to particular actions or general actions?

4. Do happiness or interests refer to people's own understanding of their interests and/or preferences or what we think is in their best interest or will make them happy.

Example 1: Umberto, the plastic surgeon

Utilitarianism says that Umberto should continue with his job because the happiness of others should come first, especially when it is the majority

Umberto is a plastic surgeon specialising in the repair of birth defects. He lives in a part of the country where there is no-one else with his skills and qualifications. Umberto has two children, whom he sees very little of because he spends long hours at the hospital. He is a nice father and his children want to see more of him. He would not earn significantly less money if he decided not to work at weekends and to take holidays with his children. And his children would be happier. But hundreds of other children would then not get the operations that they need in order to live normal lives.

(Adam Morton, 'Teaching Philosophy', *Cogito*, Spring 1994, p. 76)

Example 2: Marietta's uncle

Utilitarianism says that Marietta should let the uncle overdose because then his will & money will benefit more people (the majority)

Marietta looks after her old uncle who has become mean and miserly, and wants to change his will. In his more generous days, he had bequeathed a vast sum of money to a charity which supports both cancer research and the provision of hospices for children with terminal cancer. This money would be of great benefit in helping to find a cure for childhood cancers, and in making the lives of those who cannot be cured much happier. But the uncle has decided to leave his money instead to his estranged son who lives abroad, is already rich, and is much less generous than his father. The uncle is very forgetful about his medication, and often would take an overdose if Marietta did not stop him. He has arranged to see his solicitor to change his will. On the night before this meeting is due to take place, Marietta sees him about to take an additional dose of medication, which she knows will be fatal. If he dies in the night, the money will go to the charity, and the lives of many children will be made happier.

Utilitarianism says that Sam should give the money to the people (the majority) rather than using it for herself.

Example 3: Sam and famine relief

Having recently graduated with a degree in social studies, Sam has landed a very well paid job. She has no dependants, enjoys life very much, and would like to use her new found affluence in order to travel whenever possible, to buy a car, to go to the theatre often, and to eat at expensive restaurants. But she sees an appeal on television for donations to famine relief, and begins to think that she should forgo some of her pleasures in order to increase the happiness of people in other parts of the world. How much should she give? How many of the people who are suffering does she have to worry about. Does she have to think about the welfare of future generations, as well as the welfare of people alive now?

Umberto must maximise the satisfaction of the preferences of everyone affected by the amount of time he spends on his job. If he spends less time on his job, hundreds of children will not get what they would prefer – their birth defects remedied by Umberto's skills in plastic surgery. If he continues to spend the same amount of time, or even more time on his job, his own two children will not get what they would prefer – to spend more time with their father. More preferences will be satisfied if Umberto continues to work at weekends, so the utilitarian principle tells him that that is what he should do.

Is there a problem with this recommendation? Well, we can certainly identify something which would pull Umberto in the other direction, and this would not just be a *wish* to consider the interests of his own children, but a sense that he has a *moral obligation* to regard his own children's interests as a very high priority. The utilitarian principle does not allow him to give more weight to the interests of those closest to him. In Jeremy Bentham's words, 'Each person is to count for one, nobody for more than one'. So utilitarianism has difficulty allowing for special moral obligations associated with roles such as those of parent, brother, sister and so on.

What must Marietta do, according to the utilitarian principle? More preferences will be satisfied if she allows her uncle to take the overdose of medicine, thereby preventing him from changing his will in such a way that the cancer charity will not benefit from his wealth. But would this be the right thing to do? Wouldn't it be unfair to her uncle to let him take an

Utilitarianism aims to maximize interests or preferences

accidental overdose, if she would not have treated another elderly person, whose death could not have benefited others, in the same way? The problem for utilitarianism highlighted by this example is that the principle of maximising preferences can result in some people's preferences, even for such important things as freedom and continued existence, being denied in the interests of a larger group.

What does the utilitarian principle tell Sam that she must do about contributions to famine relief? She needs to find out how her contributions would be used, and the extent to which others would benefit. But certainly she must consider the satisfaction of the preferences of people all over the world, and it is likely that more preferences will be satisfied if she gives a large percentage of her income to charity, and does not satisfy her own preferences for a relatively luxurious life. Does she have to consider the preferences of future generations of people? Nothing in the principle rules this out. If more people will be born, and will have preferences, then these preferences will have to be taken into account.

The implications of the utilitarian principle begin to seem too demanding when we realise that it obliges us to take account of the entire world and future generations, even if we have not been wondering, like Sam, whether we should contribute to famine relief. Perhaps utilitarians can modify their principle in such a way as to restrict the preferences we should take into account to those of our immediate neighbourhood, or social group, or country. Or maybe the implication that we have very wide obligations is correct, and our tendency to regard the principle as too demanding is due to selfishness or limited sympathy. We leave you to think about this. However, whichever conclusion is correct, there is still a problem for utilitarianism in relation to our obligations to future generations. If one's own country, or the world, could provide a comfortable life for a larger population than at present, then it is likely that more preferences could be satisfied if the population were increased. This suggests that not only should we try to maximise satisfaction of preferences of those who happen to be born in the future, we should also try to maximise the number of people born who would then have preferences which we could satisfy. This would generate a moral requirement to produce children, rather than it being left to individuals to choose the size of their family. This rather odd implication could be avoided if the utilitarian principle were to read: 'Act so as to produce maximum satisfaction of preferences of those now alive who will be affected by your action'. However, this restriction would mean that we did not need to worry about the effects, for example, of pollution or of exhaustion of resources on future generations, and perhaps we should worry about such things.

Can the principle be modified in order to deal with the problems raised by Examples 1 and 2 – i.e. the difficulty of allowing for special responsibilities such as those of parents, and the suggestion that utilitarianism cannot safe-guard justice? The standard response by utilitarians is to say that reference to moral rules must be incorporated into the principle. Instead of recommending that we should simply perform the action which produces the best conse-quences, they recommend that we should follow the rules of conduct which, if they were followed by all, would generally produce the best consequences. This is a move from what is called act-utilitarianism to what is called rule-utilitarianism. The rule-utilitarian principle would be: 'Act in accordance with the rules of conduct which tend to produce maximum satisfaction of preferences'. (As we said earlier, this seems to be what Mill's principle recom-mends.) The rule-utilitarian will point out that most people will prefer to have rules of conduct which require parents to give greater priority to the interests of their own children, and which forbid treating some people badly in order to improve the fortunes of others. Most people will prefer a rule which safeguards justice, because they would feel insecure and fearful if there were no such rule.

Whilst avoiding some of the pitfalls of act-utilitarianism, rule-utilitari-anism runs into its own problems. One criticism is that it isn't really utilitarian, because it has acknowledged that maximising the satisfaction of preferences might not be the most important consideration. In Marietta's case, for example, no-one will know if she fails to prevent her uncle's death, so this particular flouting of the rule will not lead to general insecurity. Yet rule-utilitarianism would require her to save her uncle, and thereby satisfy fewer preferences, so that it seems to be inconsistent with the basic idea of utilitarianism. This, of course, does not necessarily mean that it is a mistaken theory – simply that it is radically different from act-utilitarianism.

Another problem is that it seems to give the wrong sort of justification for treating people justly. For example, if Marietta should not let her uncle take an overdose, then it seems mistaken to say that the reason for this is that it is required by a rule which satisfies the preferences of most people. Shouldn't she treat him justly even if the preferences of others would not require this?

Utilitarianism and moral concepts

How does the utilitarian principle relate to some of the concepts which have come up in our examples of arguments and decisions in earlier chapters? Utilitarianism is clearly related to the concept of harm, and the idea that there is something wrong with causing harm to others, though it goes beyond that to imply that we should make positive efforts to produce beneficial outcomes for others. It stresses the idea of beneficence – doing positive good. Yet it may have to permit harm to some individuals in order to benefit a majority.

REALLY important to remember

Its relationship with some of the other concepts we have considered, for example, justice, rights and autonomy is less direct. The concept of rights could be derived from rule-utilitarianism, as follows. We will probably find that most people are happier if there is general observance of a rule which implies that human beings have certain rights, some of which will be protected by law. So your having the moral right to life, or the moral right to liberty is justified by the fact (if there is such a fact) that preferences will be maximised if everyone is regarded as having these rights. The concepts of justice and of autonomy could be accommodated in a similar way by rule-utilitarianism.

[handwritten margin note:] right to life, → right to happiness

The concept of a person is not of central importance to utilitarianism, because it does not restrict moral concern to persons. Nevertheless, just as those who use the concept of a person need some view about which entities have the capacity of self-consciousness, so also does utilitarianism depend on views about the *capacities* of various entities – in this case the capacity to have preferences. So if utilitarians are to be able to settle questions about how different entities should be treated, they need to be able to say which kinds of entities can have preferences.

Kant's moral theory

Immanuel Kant, a German philosopher writing in the late eighteenth century produced a moral theory firmly opposed to the idea that the morality of an action is determined by its consequences. Consequentialist moral theories, such as utilitarianism, are often contrasted with deontological moral theories, of which Kant's theory is an example, and which insist that some actions are right and some actions are wrong regardless of their consequences. The word 'deontological' derives from the Greek word meaning 'duty'.

Kant said that the way to find out what our duties are is to apply a principle which he called the categorical imperative – 'Act only according to that maxim by which you can at the same time will that it should become a universal law' (*Groundwork of the Metaphysic of Morals*, 1785). This connects with the idea that you shouldn't act in any way in which you would be unwilling to allow everyone else to act, which reminds us that if we think it is wrong for others to behave in a certain way, we cannot consistently claim that it is morally acceptable for us to behave in that way in exactly the same circumstances. You may remember that we made the same point in Chapter 3 about Saul's decision as to whether to become a vegetarian – that if he thought that the widespread practice of meat-eating was wrong on the grounds that it involved killing animals, he could not then excuse his own meat-eating by saying 'It will make no difference to how many animals are killed if *I* give up eating meat'.

The wording of the principle may tempt us to think that Kant's theory depends on individual preferences, if we interpret 'can will' as meaning 'would be willing to allow'. This interpretation would mean, for example, that those who were willing to be treated cruelly would be morally justified in being cruel to others. However, Kant almost certainly meant 'can rationally and without inconsistency will', and he would have thought that someone who did not mind cruel treatment was irrational. There is, nevertheless, a difficulty in deriving from the categorical imperative the moral rules which Kant thought could be derived – for example, that murder, lying and breaking promises are wrong. Let us illustrate this in relation to murder. Someone contemplating murder must ask 'Can I rationally and without inconsistency will that others act in this way?' To insist that the answer must be 'no' requires an assumption that it is irrational both not to mind being murdered, and to be willing to take the risk that one may be murdered. These may be reasonable assumptions. However, the greatest problem arises when we think about how the action which the potential murderer contemplates must be described. Imagine a jealous husband who considers whether it is morally permissible to murder his wife's lover, and assume that the husband loves his wife so much that he would never become the lover of someone else's wife. Would it be irrational of him to will that all jealous husbands may murder their wives' lovers? Perhaps not, and if not then the test of the categorical imperative would imply that it would not be wrong to commit murder. But surely it would be wrong.

Kant offered another principle, called the formula of the end in itself, which he thought was simply another version of the categorical imperative. Yet, it is different, in that it makes a more specific recommendation about how we should treat other people. It says 'Act in such a way that you always treat humanity, whether in your own person or in the person of any other, never simply as a means but always at the same time as an end'. We shall concentrate on this principle, rather than the categorical imperative, because it is less abstract and thus easier to apply to examples of moral dilemmas. Indeed, the principle underlies some of the concepts used in discussions of practical ethical issues, but in order to see this we need a clear idea of what the principle means.

Clarifying the formula of the end in itself

The first thing to notice about the principle is that it tells us how we should treat 'humanity', so it has no implications for the treatment of animals. Kant himself thought that we have no direct duties to animals, and that animals exist in order to serve the ends of humans. However, we can evaluate the principle as applied to human beings without accepting Kant's own views of the status of animals. Moreover, we should note that Kant suggested that we have *indirect* duties to animals, to the extent that cruelty to animals may make us callous towards human beings.

The principle gives us two requirements; we must never treat other people 'simply as a means', and we must always treat any other person 'as an end'. In the first of these, the word 'simply' is crucial, because in many transactions in everyday life, we use others as a means to our own ends. For example, we use the shop assistant as a means to making our purchases, we use the doctor as a means to restoring our health. What is meant by using someone *simply* as a means is trying to get them to do things, for our own purposes, which they would not choose to do if they were fully informed. We do not manipulate the shop assistant and the doctor if they are carrying out their jobs voluntarily. But it is possible to manipulate others by deceiving them, and this is one of the things which the principle tells us we must not do. Another example of using others simply as a means is suggested by the story of Marietta and her uncle. Suppose Marietta had been so determined that her uncle's money should go to the cancer charity that she had decided to kill him herself in order to be absolutely certain that he could not change his will. She would then have been guilty of simply using him as a means to benefit others.

The other part of the principle is more obscure. What does it mean to say we should treat someone 'as an end'? Modern Kantians interpret this as meaning that we should not merely respect others as rational persons with aims and purposes of their own, but that we should also make some attempt to help others to achieve some of those aims. This begins to sound like the utilitarian requirement to aim to satisfy the preferences of others, but it differs in that it does not demand that we *maximise* anything. In Onora O'Neill's words: 'Kantians will claim that they have done nothing wrong if none of their acts is unjust, and that their duty is complete if in addition their life plans have in the circumstances been reasonably beneficent' ('A Simplified Account of Kant's Ethics' in *Matters of Life and Death*, ed. T. Regan 1986).

Applying the formula of the end in itself

Before reading further, think about the three examples which we considered in relation to utilitarianism. What would the formula of the end in itself tell Umberto, Marietta and Sam that they should do?

In Umberto's case, the formula offers little to help him make a decision. We can assume that since he is a nice father, and since his work gives children the help which they and their parents want, he is using neither his own children, nor his patients simply as a means to his own ends. His dilemma is that if he continues to work long hours, he will not promote his children's aim to spend more time with their father, and if he works shorter hours he will not

[handwritten margin notes:]
Must not deceive people or manipulate them

Basically, use people to their fully potential

Help others achieve their goals & purposes

promote the aim of some other children to get treatment. The principle itself cannot give an answer as to whose aims should take priority.

We have already suggested that Marietta would be acting against the formula if she killed her uncle as a means to making the lives of child cancer sufferers happier. Would she be using him as a means if she did not actively kill him, but just neglected to stop him taking an overdose? That question may be difficult to answer, but it does seem that she would be failing to treat him as an end, i.e. as a person with aims of his own. We assume that he wants to go on living, and it is clear that he wants his wealth to go to his son. By failing to stop him taking an overdose, she would be failing to help him achieve these aims.

[handwritten annotation:] ←This is because the def. does not contain "maximum" like utilitarianism

What does the formula tell Sam that she should do? She knows that there are people dying from famine. She is not doing anything to them, so she cannot be said to be using them as a means to her ends. But if she does not contribute to famine relief, is she failing to treat these people as ends? The question is difficult to answer partly because Sam never comes into contact with the people who are starving. How can we be treating people in any way at all, or even failing to treat them in a proper way, if we never meet them? Does Kant's theory have nothing to say about ethical issues concerning people with whom we have no direct contact?

In 'Kantian Approaches to Some Famine Problems', Onora O'Neill outlines a way in which Kant's formula can be seen as relevant to such issues. It contrasts with Peter Singer's utilitarian position, and in order to get a detailed understanding of this contrast, you could read O'Neill's paper and Chapter 8 in Singer's *Practical Ethics*. In that chapter, Singer sets out an argument as follows:

> First premise: If we can prevent something bad without sacrificing anything of comparable significance, we ought to do it.
>
> Second premise: Absolute poverty is bad.
>
> Third premise: There is some absolute poverty we can prevent without sacrificing anything of comparable moral significance.
>
> Conclusion: We ought to prevent some absolute poverty.

You can practise your skills of argument assessment on this example. He assumes that the contributions of individuals would make a difference to those in other countries suffering absolute poverty, and he suggests 'that those earning average or above average incomes in affluent societies, unless they have an unusually large number of dependants or other special needs, ought to give a tenth of their income to reducing absolute poverty'.

O'Neill's discussion is not so directly addressed to individuals, but she does talk about duties of beneficence in times of famine. Her view is that, because, according to Kant's theory, the most basic duty of beneficence is to put people in a position to be autonomous, and because no-one who is starving can be autonomous, the relief of famine rates high among the duties of beneficence. It is not clear whether this duty is owed principally by governments rather than individuals.

In a final section of her paper, entitled 'Lifeboat Earth', O'Neill draws what looks like a stronger conclusion. She points out that the economic interdependence of countries is now such that the lifestyles and activities of Western countries have effects on the well-being of other countries. So affluent countries cannot simply claim that in giving but little to famine relief they are meeting all the obligations that Kantian theory demands, because if our lifestyles actually cause starvation in other countries, then we are killing people in other countries (a matter of failing to be just) rather than merely failing to save them, and thereby failing to be as kind to them as we could be. This makes famine relief more an issue of justice than of beneficence.

2 concepts: Justice & autonomy

Kant's theory and moral concepts

Utilitarianism does not follow justice

The two requirements of the formula of the end in itself connect directly with two of the crucial concepts for practical ethics, namely justice and autonomy.

Our simple definition of justice in Chapter 4 was 'treating equals equally', and we have suggested that utilitarianism has difficulty in accommodating this value, since in some situations maximum satisfaction of preferences might be achieved by treating an individual or a minority group differently from the majority. Kant's formula requires that everyone be treated with equal respect as persons with aims and purposes of their own. The idea of rights does not appear in Kant's theory. His focus was on duty – what we owe to others, rather than what we are entitled to demand from others. There is, of course, some relationship between rights and duties, as we pointed out in Chapter 5. If you have a right to life, then others have a duty not to kill you. But the relationship may not work the other way round. So it is not obvious that the concept of rights can be derived from Kant's formula.

The concept of autonomy underlies Kant's theory. He thought that human beings are all potentially rational and capable of making choices about their own lives. The formula of the end in itself implies that autonomy should be respected – we should not manipulate others into doing things they would not otherwise have wished to do. O'Neill's interpretation of 'treating others as ends' also implies that autonomy should be promoted – we should make some attempt to put some others in a position to be autonomous. Kant did not explicitly introduce the concept of a 'person', but his emphasis on the importance of autonomy implies that our moral obligations are owed only to those entities which are potentially rational and autonomous.

There is a connection between Kant's theory and the concept of harm. The formula requires that we treat others as persons with aims of their own, and if we can assume that it would be contrary to anyone's aims that they should be harmed, it does suggest that we should not directly inflict harm on other people.

Yet Kant's theory does not require us to take into account all the potentially harmful consequences of our actions, since it insists that some actions are right irrespective of their consequences. One example can illuminate this. The formula generates the moral rule that we must tell the truth, since if we deceive others, we are not respecting their autonomy. In Chapter 2 we used the example of someone being asked the whereabouts of Anne Frank's family when they were hiding from the Nazis in Amsterdam. The consequences of telling the truth in this situation could include suffering and death for the members of the Frank family. But Kant's insistence that the moral rules which are derived from his principle are absolute implies that we must not lie, even if refusing to lie results in the infliction by others of terrible harm. Kant defends this stance by reminding us that we cannot be certain what the consequences of our actions will be – perhaps a lie will not have the good consequences which we predict. As we pointed out in our discussion of famine relief, Kant's theory does include the concept of beneficence – doing good to others, but it is not specific about how much good we should do and to whom.

Moral theories and some other principles

The principle that 'Killing is wrong'

The principle that killing is wrong underlies many of the arguments about ethical issues, for example abortion, euthanasia and vegetarianism, which we have encountered in earlier chapters. It also figures in discussions about the morality of capital punishment and of war. As a moral consideration, it has something in common with the concept of harm, in that it is very widely accepted, and we would think there was some moral defect in someone who simply could not see that it was a moral consideration at all – someone who said 'What's so bad about killing?' It is tempting to think that we do not even have to seek a justification for the principle. However, because the principle is so important, any moral theory which offers a supposedly over-arching moral principle should be able to justify the idea that killing is wrong by means of its own principle.

We suggested in Chapter 2 that you might attempt to assess the principle

'Killing is wrong' by thinking about its applications. You may have concluded that some exceptions need to be built into the principle. For example, it may not be wrong to kill someone who is threatening the life of another person, if that would be the only way to save the potential victim. Should this idea of the permissibility of killing in self-defence be extended to make killing in wartime morally acceptable? Could there be other exceptions to the principle, to allow, for example, abortion and euthanasia to be morally permissible? What kind of justification for the principle, and what exceptions, are implicit in the two moral theories we have examined?

Utilitarianism and 'Killing is wrong'

Utilitarians must justify the claim that killing is wrong in terms of the consequences of killing – principally that it deprives someone of a future during which their interests and preferences could have been satisfied. Act-utilitarianism cannot insist on an absolute rule against killing, because, in some circumstances the satisfaction of preferences may be maximised if some people are killed. Rule-utilitarians would justify an absolute rule against killing by pointing out that if there were no such rule, everyone would feel very insecure and fearful. Yet, there could be specific exceptions, even to an absolute rule.

Kant's moral theory and 'Killing is wrong'

Kant's theory can justify the claim that killing is wrong by means of the concept of respect for persons and for their autonomy.

To kill someone who wanted to go on living would be to fail to treat that person as someone with aims and purposes of their own.

We have said that Kant believed that moral rules were absolute, so he would not have accepted that the consequences of killing could ever justify it. However, there is room for the idea of an exception to the principle in some cases. For example, killing in self-defence could be seen as treating others in the way in which they have decided people may be treated. Interestingly, Kant uses this idea to justify capital punishment.

The doctrine of acts and omissions

In this section we ask you to consider whether some controversial cases should be exceptions to the principle that killing is wrong. Read each of the following examples, and decide whether it would be wrong to kill in these cases. If so, try to say exactly why.

Example 1: Permanent vegetative state

A young man, Tony Bland, suffered brain damage due to oxygen starvation when he was crushed against the barrier at Hillsborough football ground in April 1989. He was judged to be in a permanent vegetative state –his brain stem was alive, so that he could breathe normally, but all his higher brain function had gone, so that he could not feed himself, and had to be connected to a feeding tube in order to survive. After almost four years, his parents applied for a legal judgement to allow him to be disconnected from the feeding tube, and therefore to die. This was granted, the tube was disconnected, and he died about ten days later. At the time, his doctor said that he could see no moral difference between giving Tony a lethal injection and removing the feeding tube, but he would not do the former because it was illegal.

[handwritten margin note: utilitarianism: the removing the tube]

[handwritten margin note: Kant: the injection is better]

Example 2: Elderly Alzheimer sufferers with pneumonia

Many elderly people in nursing homes who suffer from Alzheimer's disease are not treated with antibiotics when they fall ill with pneumonia. They could be treated, and often they would recover, but a judgement is made that it is appropriate that their lives should not be prolonged in this way. The pneumonia is allowed to take its course, and death results. Would it be wrong to give a lethal injection in these circumstances?

Example 3: Infants with severe disabilities

Imagine the case of a child being born with a disability which is so severe that the child will die within a month, and there is no medical procedure which can remedy the disability. Would it be wrong to kill the child?

In the first two cases, a decision is effectively made that a life should come to an end, and in the third case the end of life is not preventable. You may have thought that in each case, it is right to let the person die, but it would not be right to kill them. Those who think that killing someone is always morally worse than letting someone die are relying on a general claim, known as the acts and omissions doctrine, which says that:

> There is a moral difference between *performing an act* which has certain consequences, and *failing to act* when that failure to act has exactly the same consequences.

You can probably see immediately that utilitarians must reject this doctrine, because it is the consequence which determines the rightness of our behaviour, so doing nothing can be just as bad as doing something. This is why utilitarianism imposes such a heavy responsibility upon us to relieve famine. Kant's theory is harder to apply to omissions than to actions, since his focus was upon how we know whether *intentional* actions are right or wrong. This was why we had difficulty deciding whether those who do not contribute to famine relief can be said to be 'treating' the starving in any way at all.

The acts and omissions doctrine seems plausible because we can think of many examples in which an omission *does* seem less bad than an action. For example, it seems morally worse to drown someone by pushing them into a river than to fail to rescue someone who has fallen into the river; and it seems morally worse to send poisoned food to people who are starving than to fail to send them food at all. But should we accept it as a general rule or principle applying to all cases? We leave you to consider this in the light of your responses to our examples.

However, the Bland case prompts an important observation about the acts and omissions doctrine – that it can be difficult to know whether someone's behaviour should be described as an act or as an omission. Tony Bland's feeding tube had to be disconnected from time to time in order to clean it. Once the decision had been made that he should be allowed to die, the tube could have been removed immediately (clearly an action). But in fact the doctor waited until the tube was next due to be disconnected, and he did not re-connect it. Was this an omission, rather than an action? And what moral difference could this distinction make?

The doctrine of double effect

We now focus on some cases of deaths which result from a particular action, rather than an omission, but which are claimed not to be cases of intentional killing, even though the person performing the action knows that death will result. Think about whether the person is doing something wrong.

Example 4: Painkilling injections

People dying from cancer are often in such severe pain that they require very large doses of pain-killing drugs. Such drugs are extremely toxic, and can bring about death earlier than the illness would have done. This practice was referred to by Melanie Phillips in her article presented in Exercise 4, where she said that doctors 'administer pain relief which might have the side-effect of hastening the death of an already dying patient', and she describes this as 'absolutely in line with a doctor's commitments to preserve life and relieve suffering'. Her comments imply that doctors acting thus are doing nothing wrong even though they know that death will result from their actions.

Example 5: Killing 'human shields'

When Saddam Hussein thinks that Western nations are likely to attack Iraq's weapons installations, he arranges for the presence of 'human shields' at these sites. Civilians will occupy the buildings in order to deter enemies from bombing them. In times of war, would it be wrong to bomb these installations in order to destroy Iraq's weapons, even though it was known that this would also kill civilians?

In the first example, the doctor kills the patient as a side-effect of an action which is aimed at relieving the patient's pain; in the second example the bomber kills the civilians as a side-effect of an action which is aimed at destroying the enemy's weapons. Should we regard these cases as instances of killing which are exceptions to the principle that killing is wrong?

The claim that there can be exceptions in such circumstances is often defended by what is called the **doctrine of double effect,** which says:

One need not be held responsible for those effects of one's actions, which, though foreseen, are not intended, provided that:

(i) the action performed is done because it will have some good effect, even though it may also have bad effects, and

(ii) one intends only the good effects and not the bad effects of the action, and

(iii) the bad effect is not the means by which the good effect is achieved.

(An example of what would be ruled out by condition (iii) would be Marietta killing her uncle as a means to the good effect of benefiting cancer sufferers. In order to justify an action by means of the doctrine, the bad effect really must be a side-effect.)

Utilitarianism has no need of this doctrine, because it judges the rightness or wrongness of actions on the basis of their consequences, and not the intentions behind them. The doctrine is likely to be used by non-consequentialists as a way of discounting what seem to be strong moral objections to certain courses of action. Should we accept the doctrine as applying to all cases in which there are bad side-effects?

You might be tempted by the doctrine because the first example looks favourable for it, in the sense that we probably wouldn't want to say that the doctor had done anything wrong in giving the injection. But perhaps that is not because it is wrong to hold the doctor responsible for hastening death, but rather because, even though he is responsible for hastening death, he is still doing the right thing, because he is reducing suffering for someone who is going to die soon anyway.

The second example may have caused more difficulty for you, and it is not clear that it satisfies condition (i) of the doctrine of double effect. Often in wartime the supposed 'good effect' aimed at is victory for one's own side rather than peace for everyone. But suppose we accepted that the aim was for peace, would it be right to bomb the weapons installations, thereby killing civilians? And if you judge that it would be right, is this for utilitarian reasons – i.e. that the consequences (for all of which the bomber is fully responsible) would be better, or because the doctrine of double effect excuses the bomber from the responsibility for the deaths of civilians?

In the following exercise, you can apply some of the principles and theories discussed in this chapter to specific ethical issues.

Exercise 8 Applying principles and theories

The tasks in this exercise could form the basis of group discussions.

1 Imagine that a friend has lent you money, and you are about to pay him back, but you know that your friend will spend this money on drugs which will damage his health. What does utilitarianism imply that you should do? What does Kant's moral theory imply that you should do? Do you think either of them gives the right answer?

2 Apply the utilitarian principle to the question as to whether animals should be used in medical research to test the toxicity of drugs.

3 The case of Dr. Nigel Cox was discussed in Melanie Phillips' article which appears in Exercise 4. He injected a patient with potassium chloride, and she died shortly afterwards. She had been suffering intolerable pain from rheumatoid arthritis, complicated by gastric ulcers, gangrene and body sores, and it was thought that she did not have very long to live anyway. She begged to be put out of her misery.

   Apply both the utilitarian principle, and Kant's formula of the end in itself to this example.

4 Does the principle that killing is wrong imply that war is wrong?

5 Think of an example from your own experience in which you have omitted to do something, and as a result something bad has happened. Does this example show that omissions are morally equivalent to acts?

Review slides for the reasons for each example

6 Apply the principle that 'Killing is wrong', together with the doctrine of double effect, to the question as to whether the termination of pregnancy is morally permissible.

1. Utilitarianism: Should not pay it back (more benefical for yourself than for friend)
Kant: Should pay it back (keeping your word)
Right answer: Not pay it back (just my personal view)

2. Utilitarianism: It would benefit more people to perform the testing on animals than not.

3. Utilitarianism: Kill the person because the patient wants it (benefical to the patient)
Kant: Killing the person is the right thing to do. (It is an injection not necessarily killing)

4. Utilitarianism: Some wars have a bad income, meaning it is not benefical, but other wars are good, meaning it was benefical.
Kant: yes, killing is wrong

Chapter 7

Fair-mindedness and the role of emotion

Opinions about ethical issues are often so strongly held that many people find it difficult to give any consideration at all to opposing views. Yet on matters of great importance to our lives, surely we should not base our judgements upon prejudice. We should be prepared to understand the views of those who disagree with us, and to attempt to judge between opposing views in an unbiased way.

Defining fair-mindedness

One writer on critical thinking, Richard Paul, has emphasised the importance of being fair-minded, and we shall give his definition of fair-mindedness. But first, think for yourself about what it means to be fair-minded about the kinds of issues which have arisen in examples and exercises in this book. You may have disagreed with the conclusions of some of the arguments you have read – but did you give fair consideration to the case which was presented? When you made your decisions on the topics in Exercise 5, were you fair-minded in evaluating the importance of the consequences of various options? Have you been fair-minded in discussions with others on these issues?

Write out your own definition of fair-mindedness, then consider the following questions. Is it possible to be fair-minded in the way in which you have defined it? Is it always a good thing to be fair-minded in this way? Is it necessary to be fair-minded in order to make good decisions on ethical issues such as abortion and euthanasia?

You may have defined 'fair-mindedness' as 'being tolerant of other people's views'. If so, how should the three questions be answered? This depends, of course, on the meaning of 'being tolerant'. If it means 'allowing expression', then it is possible to be fair-minded in this way, and in many societies it is thought to be a good thing to allow expression of all points of view. But we might allow others to express their views without in any way giving serious consideration to those views, without their playing any role in our own decisions. Perhaps some people think that fair-mindedness simply involves listening politely to other people, on the grounds that politeness is a good thing, but that it does not require that we give any weight to other people's views.

On the other hand one might understand 'being tolerant' as requiring us to give equal weight to all points of view, in which case we would have to take the opposing point of view just as seriously as we take our own point of view. This may be possible, and in some situations it may be required. For example, some social workers believe that they should be 'non-judgemental' in their work, so that in cases where there are disputes within families, they should make no judgement as to who has right on their side. However, when we consider the third question as to whether fair-mindedness is necessary in order to make good decisions, we can see that if fair-mindedness means giving equal weight to all points of view, it is a recipe for never coming to a decision. Moreover, it does not seem to be a good thing always to give equal weight to all points of view, since the weight we should give to a point of view ought to depend upon how reasonable a point of view it is. A recent television documentary included an interview with a young man who had stolen from old people, gaining entry to their houses by posing as an official from the water company or the gas company. He apparently believed that it was morally acceptable for him to do this, in order to fund his drug habit, even though he said he would be deeply resentful if anyone treated his grandparents in this way. It may be important to *understand* his point of view, if we want to influence his future behaviour. But it is not a point of view which should be given equal weight to the view that no old people should be treated in this way.

If fair-mindedness is neither mere politeness nor acceptance that any point of view is as good as any other, how should it be defined?

Richard Paul's definition

In his book, *Critical Thinking*, Richard Paul defines 'moral fair-mindedness' as follows:

FAIR-MINDEDNESS AND THE ROLE OF EMOTION

> Willingness and consciousness of the need to entertain all moral view-points sympathetically and to assess them with the same intellectual standards without reference to one's own feelings or vested interests, or the feelings or vested interests of one's friends, community, or nation; implies adherence to moral standards without reference to one's own advantage or the advantage of one's group.
>
> (R. Paul, 1990, p. 189)

One aspect of fair-mindedness which this definition emphasises is that you must assess your own moral viewpoint according to the same standards by which you assess those of others – that is to say that you must be self-critical. It also stresses the need to make judgements without reference to one's own interest and advantage. These are crucial aspects of fair-mindedness. It is possible, though often difficult, for us to think in this way, and it is necessary if we want to make decisions which are not biased, which do not merely reflect our own personal best interests. The idea of making moral judgements without reference to one's own interest and advantage is a feature also of John Rawls' theory of justice, which we have mentioned briefly in previous chapters. Rawls maintains that certain principles of justice would emerge from the deliberations of rational beings who were placed behind a 'veil of ignorance' with respect to their own position in society and their own talents and abilities.

Paul's definition implies also that we shall not be fair-minded unless we assess moral viewpoints without reference to our own *feelings*. Can we 'adhere to moral standards' without reference to our own feelings? You will remember that in Chapter 4 we pointed out that we have to have some values in order to make decisions, otherwise there would be no way of judging between options. The crucial moral values which we identified there were the prevention of harm, respect for autonomy, and justice. Could we hold these values without *feeling* that the suffering and dignity of others provide reasons for our own actions? It seems that the commitments to avoid causing harm and to respect autonomy are dependent upon emotional responses to other people. If we did not have sympathy for others, we wouldn't care about whether our actions caused harm to others.

This point was recognised by the philosopher David Hume, writing in the eighteenth century, but Hume thought that because moral judgements are dependent upon emotional responses, reason can play only a subsidiary role in ethical decisions – helping us to work out the best means to achieve some moral end which is identified by a 'moral sense'. Kant, by contrast, thought that we can reason about morality, but that emotion must play no part in this reasoning. What the two have in common is the belief that reason and

[Handwritten margin notes: "← Don't judge others different from yourself" and "Values which we have"]

145

emotion are two entirely separate and independent activities of the human mind.

Yet, when you did Exercise 5, your reasoning about the ethical issues would have been dependent upon your concern for the welfare of others – human beings and other animals. Some people say that emotion clouds judgement on these issues. This *can* happen, and it is something we need to guard against when assessing moral viewpoints. But this does not mean that we have to become emotionless in order to be fair-minded. The crucial point is that we should not make moral judgements simply on the basis of our own unexamined feelings. We need to think about whether our emotional responses are appropriate to the situation. We also need to consider whether our emotions conflict with the important moral values. For example, if we are tempted to disregard someone's distress simply because of a feeling of dislike for that person, then we should remember that this would conflict with our commitment to justice.

In summary, Paul's definition of fair-mindedness reminds us that in making moral judgements we must assess our own views and others' views by the same intellectual standards, and we must try to eliminate bias in our own position. However, his definition also suggests that in order to be unbiased, we must ignore feelings. By contrast, we have suggested that we should deal with the problem of potential bias, not by attempting to eliminate emotion completely, but by assessing whether our emotions are appropriate. We can answer our three questions about fair-mindedness as follows:

> Is it possible to be fair-minded? Yes, in that we can strive to assess all views by the same standards, and to assess whether our own feelings are appropriate. Some examples of assessing the appropriateness of emotion will be given later in this chapter.
>
> Is it a good thing to be fair-minded, and is it necessary to be fair-minded? These two questions can be answered together, since it is a good thing *because* it is necessary in order to ensure that we do not overlook considerations which are relevant to making a decision. We shall illustrate this with some examples in the final section of this chapter.

Emotion and morality

Since our discussion of fair-mindedness has led on to comments about the proper role of emotion in ethical decisions, it will be useful to set out briefly the underlying view of the nature of emotion, and the role of some emotions in morality.

This view sees emotions not as irrational disturbances in a person's normally rational way of thinking, but as ways of perceiving the world, which can often be accurate perceptions, and which involve strong tendencies to act. For example, anger is a perception of having been badly treated, which involves the tendency to retaliate, and fear is a perception of something as dangerous, which involves the tendency to try to avoid the danger. As perceptions of various kinds of harm and benefit, emotions are useful, and play a crucial role in our reasoning processes, because they tell us what matters, what is worth acting upon. However, such perceptions can be mistaken. For example, the person with whom one is angry may not have intended to cause harm, and since the expression of anger towards someone can have serious repercussions, it is important for us to know whether the emotion is appropriate in the circumstances.

Some emotions seem to have a clear connection with morality. The idea that avoiding harm to others can provide a justification for ethical decisions is connected with an emotional response of sympathy towards people who are harmed, of wanting to help them. However, perhaps surprisingly, the emotion of resentment can also be seen as connected with moral judgements. We need to say something about the nature of morality in order to make this clearer.

Morality is not just a matter of being sympathetic to those who suffer harm. It also involves making critical judgements, both of our own and of others' actions – objecting to the actions of those who cause harm. It is easy to understand why we object to harm to ourselves – we find it unpleasant. It is difficult to see why we would react to harm to others, if we didn't care about the welfare of others, if we didn't have a tendency to sympathise with them. But the characteristic human reaction to harm is not just a tendency to help the afflicted, it involves also an objection to the person who causes the harm. This is where moral judgements connect with the emotion of resentment, which is a hostile reaction to those who are perceived as deliberately inflicting undeserved harm on others. Our practices of blame and punishment can be seen as related to this tendency.

These are not the only emotions which will figure in our moral deliberations, but they do play a central role in morality. In order to make moral judgements, we do not need to try to become like computers, removing all tendencies to experience sympathy and resentment, but we do need to know whether in a particular situation, they are the appropriate emotions to feel.

Emotion and fair-mindedness

In this section we shall discuss two ways in which emotion and fair-mindedness are connected; first that fair-mindedness requires that we assess the appropriateness of our own emotions, and second that fair-mindedness can require that we understand the emotions of others.

Fair-minded judgement of our own emotions

We have suggested that in order to be fair-minded when we make decisions we do not have to get rid of all emotion. Even if it were possible for human beings to do this, it would not be helpful, since it would leave us with no basis for making moral judgements. Instead we must consider which emotions are appropriate, and in some cases sympathy will very obviously be appropriate.

For example, in relation to a case of severe child abuse, the emotional responses of sympathy for the victim and anger towards the perpetrator, assuming that this person was capable of controlling his or her actions, are appropriate. The questions which you need to ask yourself in relation to these emotions are, in the case of sympathy – 'is the person really harmed?', and in the case of anger – 'is the perpetrator really responsible for causing harm?'.

Imagine that you are a social worker who has to investigate an allegation of child abuse. Your initial response on hearing about the case may be one of overwhelming sympathy for the child, and you question whether you are being fair-minded. What you need to know in order to make a decision about the child's future – whether, for example, to remove her from her home – is whether she has been abused or is in great danger of being abused. This alone will not settle the question as to how the social worker should act, for two reasons. First, there are different ways in which people can act sympathetically, and it may not be appropriate for a social worker to act in the same way as a sympathetic parent – for example, by effusively expressing sympathy for the child. Second, the social worker must weigh the harm the child would suffer by staying where she is against the harm which it would do to remove the child from her home. But the assessment as to whether sympathy is appropriate provides part of the information which the social worker needs in order to make a decision.

In such a case, the question 'Is sympathy appropriate?' does not mean 'If she has been harmed, is she deserving of sympathy?' It means 'Has she been harmed?' Yet in some cases of harm, sympathy may not be appropriate, for example if someone has been harmed through their own negligent actions. The appropriate reaction towards a drunken driver who injures himself may be resentment rather than sympathy, because of the harm he could have caused to others.

Assessments about the appropriateness of emotions may be required in order to make decisions on some of the topics you have thought about in earlier exercises and examples. You may have been opposed to abortion on the basis of feelings of sympathy for the foetus, or you may have been against fox-hunting because you feel sorry for foxes. What you need to assess in these cases is whether the foetus is harmed by abortion and whether the fox is harmed by the fox-hunt. You may think it is obvious that they are, because in both cases death occurs. You need to think about whether death can be harmful to entities which cannot be aware that they are being deprived of future existence (and, of course, whether foetuses and foxes lack this awareness). You need also to consider any suffering which occurs during the process of killing. Some of those in favour of fox-hunting claim that the fox enjoys the chase, and recently scientists who specialise in understanding how the brain works have reported that up to 26 weeks into a pregnancy, the foetus' brain is insufficiently developed for it to experience pain.

Sometimes emotion can stand in the way not simply of making a fair-minded judgement about a situation, but also of properly understanding what someone is saying about an ethical issue. We can illustrate this with the following extract from a recent newspaper report.

> Doctors' leaders yesterday condemned an expert on medical ethics who called for babies with severe disabilities to be given lethal injections to end their lives.
>
> Professor Peter Singer, deputy director of the Centre for Human Bioethics at Monash University in Australia, said that in cases where doctors and parents agreed that a baby's disabilities were so overwhelming as to be incompatible with a decent quality of life, it would be kinder to end the baby's life deliberately rather than leave it to die.
>
> 'The standard practice is to withhold treatment such as antibiotics or in some cases feeding so the babies do die either from untreated infections or from starvation and dehydration', he said on Radio 4's *Today* programme.
>
> 'I think that is cruel and inhumane. It causes unnecessary suffering to the infants and their families. Once you make a decision that the baby dies you ought to be able to make sure that it dies easily and swiftly. That means by giving it a lethal injection.'
>
> The Royal College of Paediatrics and Child Health said that although there were cases in which it might be appropriate to withhold or withdraw treatment there was no justification for killing children. Guidelines on when to withhold or withdraw treatment were issued by the college last year.
>
> Professor Richard Cook, consultant neo-natalogist and spokesman for the college, said: 'What I feel about people who want to bump patients off is that they are doing it for themselves. It is very difficult for doctors faced with patients for whom they can do nothing surrounded by parents and nurses who are distressed. The easiest thing is to bump them off. I don't think that is the right thing to do.'
>
> (*Independent*, 14 May 1998)

We are not using this example in order to make a judgement on the issue which is being discussed, but in order to show how strong emotional reactions can blind us to what someone is actually saying. Peter Singer makes his position clear – that when it has been decided that a disabled baby should not be treated, the baby's life should be ended *for its own sake* in order to end its suffering. Professor Cook expresses the view that anyone who wants to kill a patient wants to do so to make things easier for themselves. He is, of course saying this about doctors, not about Singer. But many doctors may share Singer's views, and may offer the same reasoning. It may be that Professor Cook's strong revulsion to the idea of killing babies would make him fail to be fair-minded by not engaging with the argument being presented. If he wishes to refute the views of Singer, he needs to try to do so not by suggesting that anyone with those views has the wrong motivation, but by showing that killing the baby would not be in the baby's interests, or that even if it would be better for the baby there is some other reason why killing is wrong, even though withholding treatment is not.

Singer's views on this topic have often been misrepresented, possibly because of strong emotional reactions against killing the innocent and helpless. He is sometimes interpreted as claiming that all disabled babies should be killed, but this is not what he is saying. The example should remind us to listen to what our opponents are saying, and engage with their arguments, rather than dismissing them simply because we feel revulsion at their apparent conclusions.

Fair-minded understanding of the emotions of others

One way in which we can fail to be fair-minded is to fail to take account of the points of view of others. This can happen not simply because we are unsympathetic, but because we fail to understand how others feel. It can, for example, be extremely difficult to judge whether others are suffering when their suffering involves no physical pain or injury, but consists in how they feel about a particular situation. It would not be fair-minded to simply dismiss or discount the claims of individuals or groups who say that certain actions or practices cause them psychological distress or are an affront to their dignity. If decisions on ethical issues sometimes require us to weigh harms, then we need to understand how those affected by a decision feel, in order to be able to gauge the extent of harm which they may suffer.

What is required is an attempt to feel what it would be like to be the other person, or a member of a group other than your own. This is undoubtedly difficult. Sometimes fiction, in the form of novels, plays and films, can be a powerful tool in enabling us to understand the emotions and perspectives of others. It is possible also to gain insight from television documentaries in which individuals describe their situation – a relatively recent example being a series about the American civil rights movement which fought against racial discrimination. A strategy which can be used in educational settings is role-play. If you have to act out the part of a member of a supposedly disadvantaged group, you may be better able to understand the extent to which members of that group suffer harm. These are ways of trying to engage our emotions in such a way that we understand the perspectives of others. Rather than being an obstacle to fair-minded assessment of ethical issues, such emotional understanding is necessary to making well-informed ethical decisions. We mention below some examples in which this kind of understanding is important.

Our first example concerns the freedom to express opinions, a freedom which we expect to be protected in our society. Yet, the Race Relations Act of 1976 sets some restriction on freedom of expression, when it says that it is an offence to use 'words which are threatening, abusive or insulting in a case where…hatred is likely to be stirred up against any racial group'. A conviction for this offence would be possible without proof that anyone suffered actual physical harm as a result of someone's 'threatening, abusive or insulting' words. Suppose you were asked to decide whether this restriction of freedom of expression was morally justified. You would have to judge whether the harm caused by this restriction of freedom was outweighed by the harm to members of different racial groups – including both the risk of physical harm, and the suffering experienced through the public expression of threats, abuse and insults. In order to make this judgement, you would need to understand how it feels to be the object of such threats, abuse and insults.

Similarly, if you wanted to decide whether it is right to censor pornographic books, magazines, films and so on, you would need to be able to compare the harm which publication of such material causes with the harm of censorship. It is often claimed that pornography is degrading to women, and an important aspect of your deliberation would be attempting to understand this claim – to feel what it is like to be a woman in a society in which pornography is not censored.

We are not claiming that people's feelings should always be the deciding factor, nor indeed that they should always carry weight in the ethical decision – rather that we need to understand them in order to decide the extent to which they should be taken into account. An example of feelings which would not carry weight would be feelings of revulsion amongst white people when they first had to share facilities with black people when racial integration was introduced in South Africa. We would be right to discount such feelings, even though strongly felt, as inappropriate in relation to fellow human beings.

The issues of abortion and euthanasia can require us to understand the emotions of others. If you think that settling the question about the moral permissibility of abortion requires weighing harm to the foetus against harm to the pregnant woman, then you need to understand women's perspectives on the issue. Pregnancy and childbirth are not merely potentially painful and inconvenient interludes in a woman's life. They profoundly change one's life, and can involve great emotional distress, even if the 'solution' for someone who does not want to bring up a child is to give birth to the child and have it adopted. The emotions of the potential father may need to be considered also.

A decision to legalise voluntary euthanasia could be seen as requiring doctors to be prepared to kill their patients, which may be repugnant to some doctors. We need to understand the emotional impact of what we are asking doctors to do – if we could not do this ourselves in the same situation, should we be asking doctors to do it? In 1995 a television programme showed the mercy killing of the patient of a Dutch doctor. It was a deeply moving film, and offered viewers the chance to get an emotional grasp on the process of euthanasia. Perhaps we need this kind of emotional understanding of the issue in order to know that our decisions are justified.

We have outlined some of the ways in which emotions play a legitimate part in our fair-minded deliberations on ethical issues. You should keep this aspect of understanding in mind as you work through the final two exercises.

Exercise 9 Assessing issues in a fair-minded way

Each of the following passages concerns an issue which provokes strong feelings and conflicts of opinion. Try to assess each issue in a fair-minded way. One way to do this is to discuss the issue with someone with whom you disagree.

1 Pat Walsh on religion and the right to life.

> A 29-year-old woman in New York, who has been in a coma for 10 years, has been found to be pregnant by an as yet unidentified rapist. If no-one intervenes, she will give birth in May. The horrifying fact of the rape of an utterly defenceless and vulnerable woman is currently sending shockwaves through the United States.
>
> A potentially greater source of consternation, though, is the ethical conundrum: is it morally acceptable to allow a child conceived and brought to term in such circumstances to be born?

In the United States, some doctors and ethicists are arguing that to use a woman's body to produce a child, when she has clearly not consented to the pregnancy in the first place, is an affront to her humanity. Such a course of action is said to reduce her to the state of a 'vessel' or object, used for someone else's purposes. However, the parents of the raped woman are refusing to contemplate an abortion because they are strongly Catholic, as their daughter was, and because, understandably enough, they now see an opportunity of continuing the link with their child through the birth of her child. The fact that the child would grow up unable to communicate with her mother and without the comfort of a loving father, but merely the highly distressing knowledge that her unknown father was a creature of obscene violence, is not something that the prospective grandparents appear to have taken into account.

The moral difficulties presented by this grotesque and tragic case are as disturbing and problematic as the emotional implications, but they are not new. In April last year the case of Karen Battenbough, who was pregnant and in a persistent vegetative state, brought very similar issues to public attention. In that case doctors had decided, at the express wish of the father, to try to keep her baby alive until it was capable of independent survival. Their decision was also characterised as a violation of a woman's right not to have her body used for another's benefit. Indeed it was described by some as a case of a baby 'growing in the grave'.

Whether allowing a child to develop inside the womb of a permanently unconscious woman *is* somehow a violation of her dignity as a person is something we have to decide rather than find out. If we should come to regard such cases in that light then that judgement about pregnant comatose women will apply whether they are victims of rape or not. What is unusual about the current American case is that it is the parents who are insisting that no abortion should take place, in circumstances where perhaps most of us would expect them to be revolted by the extra wrong done to their already irreparably damaged daughter.

However, in cases where the consent of a patient to a proposed course of action cannot be obtained it is established practice to consult the views of those closest to him or her as to what the patient would have wanted. In the case of Tony Bland, for instance, where the courts were trying to decide whether it was permissible to withdraw artificial feeding and hydration from an irretrievably unconscious patient, the view of his parents that he would not have wanted to be kept alive in the circumstances was crucial. There seems no reason to think that the comatose victim of rape would disagree with what her parents say she would want. Emotional, gut reactions aside, it is therefore unclear why we should dispense with established practice –even though we f ind it extremely hard to stomach.

(Independent, 1 February 1996)

2 The relative value of mice and men

Polly Toynbee

Today the Nobel prizes are handed out in Stockholm City Hall. To coincide with the awards, a poll of all living medical Nobel laureates has been held and its results are now published.

It is surprising to find unanimity amongst scientists, but according to the poll all these distinguished medical researchers are agreed: the use of animals in research has been vital to medical progress and continues to be so.

A British patients' group called Seriously Ill for Medical Research asked all living laureates in medicine and physiology for their views on the use of animals in medical research. 100 per cent of them agreed with these statements: 'Animal experiments have been vital to the discovery and development of many advances in physiology and medicine', and 'Animal experiments are still crucial to the investigation and development of many medical treatments'.

The Seriously Ill for Medical Research group is a tough bunch of campaigners, all 400 of them suffering from incurable diseases. They fear that the animal rights campaigners are increasingly endangering medical research that might find a cure for their illnesses. Founder and director of the campaign is 34-year-old Andrew Blake, who suffers from the wasting disease Friedreich's ataxia. The treasurer has multiple sclerosis and the chair is mother of a child with cystic fibrosis. The group is backed by Stephen Hawking and other distinguished scientists. Andrew Blake sets out to counter the arguments of 'animal rights activists peddling pseudo-scientific nonsense attempting to persuade the public, at the expense of seriously ill patients, that animal research is not necessary'.

However, this group's direct interests in the success of medical research has not protected them from the extreme animal rights activists. Andrew Blake regularly receives threats, a recent one of which read, 'Your support for vivisection makes you a target. You have been warned.' But they have not been intimidated and they offer support to those researchers under direct attack; there are some 1000 animal rights attacks a year.

Recently Dr. David White, an immunologist who works on the current best hope for transplants, has been a target. He breeds pigs with a human gene which may produce an unlimited supply of organs for transplantation. His home has been wrecked three times and a hose pipe put through a skylight, so water poured through the house for a whole weekend. The whereabouts of his laboratory is now a deadly secret.

The press has often stirred up hatred of animal researchers – a part of our deeply anti-science culture. The *Sun* once printed a double-page spread with the names of animal researchers, including that of Professor Terry Partridge. He says: 'It printed who we were and where we could be found, and grossly misrepresented our work on muscle disease, saying we used animals unnecessarily. We do use mice with muscular dystrophy for our research, because we have to.'

Britain has the most stringent laws in the world on laboratory animals – laws forced on to the statute books by animal lobbyists. As a result, much important animal research is now going abroad, where it is easier to work, although Britain has always excelled in developing new drugs. The 1986 Animals (Scientific Procedures) Act has had 20 different codes of practice and guidelines added to it since it was passed, seriously impeding research. Ten of these have come into force in the last two years because of heightened animal rights pressure. Enforcing the regulations have cost research establishments and universities some £800 million – money that should have been spent on research itself. The bureaucracy is appalling. It takes months to get a permit, and the Home Office requires a monthly report. All projects need three separate licences. Then the lab has to be licensed with trained keepers and a vet on call. Each scientist has to take compulsory training, and an exam, to get another licence.

Professor Colin Blakemore has been a frequent target because he has dared to defend animal experimentation publicly. He says that the most distinguished Nobel laureates are no longer allowed to come over to Britain to collaborate on projects because they are not licensed by these new stringent rules –and they can hardly be asked to tak e exams on British regulations.

The membership and support for the British Union of Anti-Vivisectionists, the National Anti-Vivisection Society and others continues to rise, and these groups exert ever-growing political influence. All the parties have armed themselves with pro-animal statements and policies for the next election. The Conservatives boast that they introduced 'the toughest controls on animal experimentation in Europe', and the party promises that it is working hard to add a protocol on animal welfare to the Treaty of Rome.

Labour promises yet more regulation: 'We will support a Royal Commission to review the effectiveness and justification of animal experiments and to examine alternatives'. They also promise what they call 'the three Rs: reduction in the number of animals used, refinement to cut down their suffering, and their replacement whenever possible with non-animal methods'. Ominously, Labour promises 'significantly increased inspection'.

Dr. Peter Doherty collects his Nobel prize today for work on the immune system, working towards a cure for cancer, Aids and diabetes. He has to use transgenic mice in his work, and says so publicly: 'There is no alternative to the use of animals for analysing the complexity of immunity.' The logo for the Seriously Ill for Medical Research group shows a scale with a human on one side and a mouse on the other. The danger is that the scales have tipped too far in favour of the mouse.

(*Independent*, 10 December 1996)

3 In April 1995, Nicholas Ingram was executed in Atlanta, Georgia for murder, after spending 11 years on Death Row. The case received much publicity in Britain, because although Ingram had lived in the USA since early childhood, he was born in Britain, and had dual nationality. Much of the comment in British newspapers was critical of the use of capital punishment.

The murder for which Ingram was convicted took place during a robbery, in which a man and his wife were tied to a tree and shot. The wife survived, and said they had begged the gunman not to shoot them. Ingram claimed that he did not remember the murder, because he was suffering from an alcoholic blackout.

At one stage, Ingram was prepared for the electric chair, then granted a stay of execution. The following is a written statement which he made during this interval.

At around 5.30pm last night I was taken from my cell in the hospital section to H-5, the cell by the chair. I had to walk by the chair which was covered by a sheet. I was sweating it, because walking by really brought it home.

Apparently, at 5.55pm my case was stayed, but nobody told me. Indeed, at 6.20pm – the time I know because the guards told me – they began seriously to prepare me for execution. It was devoid of humanity, a bunch of sick people who apparently volunteered for the job, acting like I was an animal, a sheep being prepared for slaughter.

They shaved my head with electric shears. That was not short enough so they used a Norelco-type triple razor to cut it short , and to shave my right shin. I knew Lieutenant Stewart, an officer who used to work on death row, and Officer Kelly, a transport officer, who were doing it. They seemed like they had done it before. They treated me like an animal, and said it was just a job. They had me put on some pants with a cut up the leg for where they would attach the electrode.

They asked me what I wanted for a last meal. I said I did not want food, but I did want some cigarettes. They said the new policies forbid smoking. The chaplains were there most of the time – even befor e, when they put a finger up my anus in the strip naked 'physical' exam. They would not do anything about all this, but were trying to get me to accept their beliefs. I have my own strong religious feelings and did not want a philosophical debate with them.

They have told me it all starts again at 4pm today with the 'physical' once more, and that I am to die tonight at 7pm.'

4 On 12 March 1986, Clare Short MP presented a Bill to parliament, with the following introductory speech.

I beg to move, that leave be given to bring in a Bill to make illegal the display of pictures of naked or partially naked women in sexually provocative poses in newspapers.

This is a simple but important measure. I stress that I should like the rule to apply to newspapers and only newspapers. If some men need or want such pictures, they should be free to buy appropriate magazines, but they have no right to foist them on the rest of us.

It is said that we are free not to buy such newspapers, but things are not as simple as that. I have received several letters from women whose husbands buy such newspapers. Those women object strongly to those newspapers and object to them being left lying around the house for their children to see.

I have also talked to teachers, including my brother. He asks children to bring newspapers to school for use in discussing current affairs or for making papier mâché, and so on. Both he and the children are embarrassed by the children's reaction to the Page 3 pictures.

A precedent for my Bill can be found in the Indecent Displays (Control) Act, which provides that public hoardings cannot show such pictures, although they are not illegal when they appear in magazines or when they are seen in private. The same reasoning applies: we should not all be forcibly exposed to them. The argument and precedent are exactly the same.

During the debate on the private Member's Bill introduced by the hon. Member for Daveyhulme, I said that I intended to introduce a Bill such as this. Since then I have received about 150 letters from all over the country. About one third of them are from men –the vast majority of whom agree with me. Of course, I received some obscene letters from men, and Mr Murdoch and those Conservative Members who keep shouting out now should know that such people support and defend Page 3.

The letters came predominantly from women, particularly young women. They stressed time and again that they did not consider themselves to be prudes but objected very strongly to such pictures. One letter came from a young woman who worked in an office. She was writing on behalf of quite a few young women. They considered themselves to be young and attractive, but every day they were subjected to men reading such newspapers in the office, and to them tittering and laughing and making rude remarks such as 'Show us your Page 3s then'. Such women feel strongly that this Bill should be enacted.

Many of the letters that I received came from mothers with small children who said that they felt that Page 3 undermined their efforts to instil decent attitudes in their children. Many of them commented time and again on the front page stories of nasty newspapers such as the

Sun. It is the nastiest. Such stories deplore some brutal rape or attack on a child. The reader then turns to Page 3 to see the usual offering.

I agree with the women who think that there is some connection between the rising tide of sexual crime and Page 3. Obviously, that is unprovable, but the constant mass circulation of such pictures so that they are widely seen by children must influence sexual attitudes and the climate towards sexuality in our society. Those pictures portray women as objects of lust to be sniggered over and grabbed at, and do not portray sex as something that is tender and private.

When future generations read that in our day about 10 million newspapers carried such pictures every day to be left around and seen by children and by lots of women who did not want to see them, they will see those pictures as symbolic of our decadent society. That is why we should take action to make them illegal.

5 Can we condemn women for profiting from surrogacy?

Polly Toynbee

It is an unsavoury business, surrogacy. However decorously it is presented, the basic fact is that a rich infertile couple pays a poor woman to bear their child. Almost always it is her own genetic child, conceived with a test tube of the buyer's sperm, so the word 'surrogate' is a serious misnomer – the child is as much hers as any other. Now occasionally an embryo created from the egg and sperm of the couple may be implanted instead.

The law cannot prevent surrogacy. How do you ban women from being impregnated by men they barely know? (It happens all the time). How do you stop a man adopting his own genetic offspring, if the mother hands it over? The law is left on the sidelines, banning middlemen from profiteering, and somewhat arbitrarily fixing the maximum price paid to the mother at £10,000, describing the money euphemistically as 'costs' and 'compensation for loss of earnings'. For a mother on social security, that is a lot of money. Without mincing words, these babies are being bought and sold.

Usually it happens behind closed doors, but the British Medical Association reckons about 100 surrogate babies are born each year. Until it comes to the adoption hearing, the state has no involvement and even then often no-one reveals what has passed. Some of these arrangements end in the bitter tears of women who regret giving away their babies, or the angry tears of would-be parents who have no legal redress if the surrogate changes her mind and keeps both baby and fee.

Now the National Health Service is to venture into these treacherous waters. The NHS will rent a womb and purchase a baby for you. It is cheaper, they say, than test-tubes. At this point what was a private, if unseemly deal between individuals becomes the direct responsibility of all us tax-paying citizens. This is state baby-farming and the moral ground feels as if it shifts uneasily beneath our feet. But why should we be queasy at the state buying poor women's babies in our name? Why shouldn't the NHS let poor couples also exploit other poor women?

There is a dubious moral squeamishness at work here. We live in a society where many of the poor, by accident, bad luck, stupidity or incompetence, have no chance of participating in the ordinary quality of life of the great majority. There is, however, absolutely no sign that tax-payers are so morally shocked that they yearn to pay more in order to fund expensive new projects to rescue the poor from their benighted lives. On social security the only thing many women have left to sell is their bodies. Some women turn to prostitution, a few to womb-renting. And why not, since we have nothing else to offer them?

By the same token, I see no valid moral argument why the poor should not sell their kidneys if they choose. Most healthy people can function perfectly well with one. The chance to earn a windfall of, say, £50,000, could make a real difference to their lives, and would seem a perfectly rational choice to make.

In fact kidney sale is a far better proposition than surrogacy, since the donors are unlikely to mourn their loss the way a mother may mourn her missing child. A hard-headed examination of the issues raised by surrogacy on the NHS may well lead down the path to NHS-purchased spare organs. It would save the lives of many kidney patients dying while they wait, and the livelihoods of the desperately poor.

(*Independent*, 15 February 1996)

Exercise 10 Using all the skills

For this final exercise, you should put to use all the skills you have been practising: questioning evidence and authorities, evaluating explanations, making assumptions explicit, drawing well-founded conclusions, clarifying ethical concepts, applying principles and coming to a definite decision on the issue.

The issues in this exercise have recurred in examples and exercises earlier in the book, so you will already have done some thinking about these matters. We now ask you to bring together these thoughts, and produce a well-argued case which answers a broad question on each topic. In Appendix 2 you will find a summary of the concepts, arguments, issues and further reading relevant to each topic, except for the topic of famine relief, which is discussed in Chapter 5.

There are a number of ways in which you might approach this exercise. It could be treated as the basis for group discussions in class, or you could write an essay on the topic. You may wish to attempt your essay before looking at Appendix 2, then check to see whether there are any important aspects which you have overlooked. Or you may prefer to use Appendix 2 and further reading to help you to write the essay or prepare for a class discussion.

1　What moral restrictions are there on the ways in which we treat animals?

2　Is abortion morally wrong? Give a justification for your answer.

3　In what circumstances, if any, is euthanasia morally justifiable?

4　Can going to war, or intervening in a war, be morally justifiable?

5　What moral restrictions are there upon the ways in which wars should be conducted?

6　Do we have moral obligations to conserve other species?

7　Should capital punishment be re-introduced in Britain? Give a justification for your answer.

8　What moral responsibilities do individuals in relatively affluent countries have towards those in other countries who suffer famine?

Appendix 1 – Comments on selected exercises

Exercise 1

1   This *could* be regarded as an argument, with the first sentence as the conclusion. However, since the first sentence doesn't do much more than summarise the comparisons made in the second sentence, it is also reasonable to say that it is not an argument. It is not a moral argument, since it does not make a moral recommendation, although the comment about animal suffering could be used to draw an evaluative conclusion about fox-hunting and angling.

2   This is an argument, and the conclusion is the first sentence. The passage tries to convince us that we should not assume that disagreement about moral issues means that there can be no rational discussion about such issues. It does this by means of a comparison with discussion on scientific matters. The argument is not a moral argument, because the conclusion is not a moral recommendation.

3   This is an argument in which the conclusion – the second sentence – is clearly signalled by the word 'Therefore'. It is not a moral argument, because it does not claim that there are moral reasons as to why we should not experiment on mice. It suggests

instead that there is no point in doing such experiments, because they would not tell us what we want to know.

4   This is a moral argument, which concludes in the second sentence that skinny models should not be criticised for presenting unhealthy images. It aims to convince us of this by mentioning two other cases about which, it is assumed, we shall agree that those who present unhealthy images should not be criticised.

5   This is not an argument, since it draws no conclusion from the comments about the potential adverse effects of pornography and violent films.

6   You may have found it difficult to identify a clear conclusion in this passage. The author certainly wants us to accept that no-one should be punished for their actions during war-time, on the grounds that if, as is widely accepted, it is not wrong to engage in war, then killing the enemy in war-time cannot be wrong. We can regard it as a moral argument since it is making a claim as to which actions are morally justifiable. You may think that the author jumps to unjustified conclusions. Ask yourself whether the argument makes some unwarranted assumptions.

7   This is not so much an argument as a description of a possible scheme for rationing energy use. Yet it is clear that those in favour of the scheme could construct a moral argument with the conclusion that this scheme should be adopted because it would have two advantages – reducing energy consumption, and redistributing wealth in a 'healthy' way.

8   This passage is clearly trying to get us to accept that tobacco companies are not to blame if smokers suffer from smoking-related illnesses. You may have thought that the main emphasis was on the other claim – that smokers themselves are to blame for their smoking-related illnesses. But it is reasonable to regard the first sentence as the main conclusion, and the last sentence as part of the reasoning which is meant to support it. Is it a moral argument? The reasoning seems to be based on non-moral considerations – smokers know the risks, and they make a choice whether or not to smoke. You may, however, wish to interpret it as a moral argument, because the passage has a tone of moral disapproval towards those who claim that others are responsible for their health problems.

9   This is a moral argument with the final sentence as the conclusion, clearly signalled by the word 'So'. The claim that rapists and arsonists should complete the full term of their prison sentence is supported by the claim that

those who are a danger to society should not be given remission even if they have behaved well in prison. Notice that the argument assumes that convicted rapists and arsonists are a danger to the public.

10   This is an argument which concludes that it is not true that embryo research will bring treatment and miracle cures. The reasons given for this claim are that testing for disorders does not help disabled people, and cannot prevent handicaps. It is reasonable to regard this as a moral argument, since the use of the word 'cruelly' implies that the impression created by embryo researchers not only is untrue, but also has adverse effects. Notice that the argument assumes that the only way in which embryo research could lead to treatment and cures would be by helping people who are now disabled and by eliminating all handicaps.

Exercise 2

2   We can regard this passage as having two independent lines of reasoning for its conclusion that

> The use of cannabis should be made legal

The first reason is that:

> it is no more harmful than other drugs – alcohol and tobacco – the use of which is legal.

The second line of reasoning is:

> the purpose of laws is to protect us from harm

This is meant to support an intermediate conclusion that:

> there is no point in having a law against the use of cannabis

There are two assumptions upon which the argument relies. In order to support the conclusion, the first reason needs an assumption that:

> The harmfulness of alcohol and tobacco is not a sufficient justification for making their use illegal,

and the second line of reasoning needs an assumption that:

The use of cannabis is not (significantly) harmful.

The passage relies on the moral concept of harm, and on the moral principle that activities should be illegal only if this protects us from harm. A clear comparison is made between the use of cannabis and the use of alcohol and tobacco.

4   The conclusion of this argument is that:

Adults should resist the temptation to be over-protective towards children.

The immediate reason given for this is that:

it has the opposite effect to that which is desired.

This claim is given support by the two other sentences in the passage – the general claim that children need to be free to make mistakes in order to learn, and the specific example about needing to learn road safety for themselves.

There is an assumption that children cannot learn about the dangers in the world if adults are protecting them from risks.

There is no specific mention of moral concepts and principles, but the argument relies on the assumption that adults should act in a way which is most beneficial for children in the long run.

6   The conclusion of this passage is that the couples who produced the frozen embryos should decide whether the embryos should be destroyed or preserved for another five years, and that the embryos of those couples who cannot be traced should be destroyed now.

The reasoning towards this conclusion is as follows:
Reason 1:

[If the rules were changed now] couples could suddenly find that against their wishes someone else was bearing and bringing up the brother or sister of their own children.

Reason 2:

That wasn't something they were warned about when they first agreed to fertility treatment.

Reason 3:

> Nor is it something they should be forced to deal with and adjust to now.

These three reasons taken jointly are intended to support the Intermediate Conclusion that:

> It would be far more unethical to change the rules now [than to destroy the embryos of those couples who cannot be traced].

The reasoning relies on the assumption that the 'pro-life' MP David Alton is wrong to regard these embryos as orphans who should be adopted. If it were correct to regard them in this way, then, if it would be wrong to destroy new-born babies whose parents could not be traced, wouldn't it also be wrong to destroy these embryos, even if to do otherwise would cause serious problems for the parents?

The argument relies implicitly on the moral concept of harm, since it bases its conclusion on the claim that there would be adverse effects for the producers of the embryos if the rules were changed. We are not given the reasoning of the 'pro-life' lobby, but their views are often defended by means of the concept of a right to life.

8 You may have found it difficult to pick out a sentence in this passage which expresses the conclusion, yet there is clearly some reasoning going on, and it is clear that the author wants us to accept that it would be wrong to reintroduce capital punishment. So we can regard this as the implicit conclusion.

The immediate reason given for this, which we can regard as an intermediate conclusion is that:

> To reintroduce it would not testify to a renewed reverence for human life; it would witness to an increased callousness about destroying it.

This claim is in turn supported in the following way.

Reason 1:

> [If we should treat people who commit violent crimes in the way they have treated others, then] we should torture those who have tortured, rape those who have raped, mutilate those who have mutilated, and kill those who have killed.

Reason 2:

> Nobody maintains this in the first three of these cases; almost everyone can see that, if doing something is abhorrent, doing it in return is likewise abhorrent.

These two reasons, taken jointly, can be seen as supporting an unstated intermediate conclusion (thus an assumption) that:

> We should not treat those who have committed violent crimes as they have treated others.

The argument does not explicitly refer to moral concepts, but does take for granted that harming others is wrong. The assumption identified above is a moral principle. There is a clear comparison between different crimes, which is intended to support the idea that our ways of punishing these crimes should rest on similar principles.

Exercise 3

Passage 1

1 *Conclusion*
The conclusion is that there should be a law against parents hitting their children.

2 *Reasons and assumptions*
There is one reason – that children are more likely to be well-behaved if parents use other kinds of punishment than physical violence.

There is an assumption that if there were a law against parents hitting their children, parents would be less likely to hit their children.

3 *Truth of reasons and assumptions*
In order to assess the truth of the reason, we would need to look at evidence from psychologists' studies of the effects of different methods of punishment by parents. In fact, some studies do report that if parents behave aggressively towards their children, children are more likely to be aggressive towards others.

The truth of the assumption is questionable since it is likely that parents would not expect it to be discovered that they were hitting their children, unless they caused obvious injury. If they did cause obvious injury, they would be guilty of child abuse, which is illegal in any case.

4 *Reliability of authorities*

The passage does not mention any authorities, but if we rely on what psychologists report we need to consider whether they are experts.

5 *Additional evidence*

We need expert evidence in order to judge which methods of punishment are most likely to produce good behaviour, so your own individual observations will not settle the question.

You may have observed that nothing has been said about whether it would be possible to enforce such a law, and such evidence would be important for trying to decide whether there should be a law.

6 *Drawing conclusions*

There are no obvious further conclusions to be drawn from the information given.

7 *Explanations*

No explanations of evidence are offered.

8 *Analogies*

There are no analogies in the passage.

9 *Strength of support of reasons for conclusion*

The major weakness in the argument is the failure to consider *all* the effects of the proposed law. Would it change the behaviour of parents? Would it be possible to find out if parents were hitting their children, without drastic levels of surveillance, which may be thought to be too intrusive? If it is true that children are more likely to be well behaved if parents do not hit them, then perhaps the most sensible recommendation would be to educate parents about the best methods of influencing children's behaviour.

Passage 3

1 *Conclusion*

The conclusion is that children should not be exposed to publicity.

2 *Reasons and assumptions*

The major claim in support of the conclusion is that publicity is habit-forming and life-changing, and requires a reasonably mature mind to grasp its implications. This claim is supported by a comparison with drinking, smoking, gambling and having sex. Michael Jackson is mentioned as one example of the supposed bad effects of making a child famous.

There is an assumption that in order to make decisions as to whether to indulge in activities which are habit-forming and life-changing, one needs a reasonably mature mind.

3 *Truth of reasons and assumptions*
The evidence for the claim that publicity is habit-forming and life-changing is simply the comparison with drinking, smoking, gambling and sex. It is likely that publicity at an early age does change a child's life, and may affect their expectations and behaviour later in life. The claim that it is habit-forming in the way that alcohol and smoking are habit-forming is more questionable. The claim that children are not mature enough to decide whether publicity would be good for them is reasonable.

4 *Reliability of authorities*
The passage does not mention any authorities.

5 *Additional evidence*
The author has mentioned one example of someone he thinks has been adversely affected by publicity during childhood. You may be able to think of others who do not appear to have been adversely affected.

6 *Drawing conclusions*
There are no obvious further conclusions to be drawn from the information given.

7 *Explanations*
No explanations of evidence are offered.

8 *Analogies*
The analogy between publicity and other activities is inappropriate in some respects. First, publicity is surely not habit-forming in the same way that smoking is habit-forming, since it does not involve an addictive substance. Second, it is not clear that publicity has similar potentially harmful results, of which the child may be unaware.

9 *Strength of support of reasons for conclusion*

The major weakness in the argument is the lack of strong evidence that publicity during childhood has harmful effects, the undesirability of which we could not expect children to be able to judge.

Paragraph 5

1 *Conclusion*
The conclusion is that the rich should leave the poor to starve.

2 *Reasons and assumptions*
There are four reasons, which are meant to support an intermediate conclusion in the following way.

Reason 1:

> We in the rich nations are like the occupants of a crowded lifeboat adrift in a sea full of drowning people.

Reason 2:

> If we try to save the drowning by bringing them aboard, our boat will be overloaded and we shall all drown.

Reason 3:

> Since it is better that some survive than none, we should leave the others to drown.

Reason 4:

> In the world today.'lifeboat ethics' apply.

These four reasons taken together are intended to support an intermediate conclusion that:

> [If the rich do not leave the poor to starve], the poor will drag the rich down with them.

There is an assumption that there are insufficient resources in the world to keep both 'rich' and 'poor' above starvation level.

3 *Truth of reasons and assumptions*

Judging whether the reasons are true essentially involves judging whether the analogy with an overcrowded lifeboat is appropriate. The important question is whether there are enough resources in the world to feed the population, without allowing starvation to reduce the population.

4 *Reliability of authorities*
The passage does not mention any authorities.

5 *Additional evidence*
What evidence could there be which would count against the conclusion? It is sometimes suggested that much more food for humans could be produced if less grain were used to feed animals for meat. Perhaps changes in eating habits could ensure the production of enough food to eliminate starvation.

6 *Drawing conclusions*
There are no obvious further conclusions to be drawn from the information given.

7 *Explanations*
No explanations of evidence are offered.

8 *Analogies*
The argument centrally depends on an analogy, but should we accept that saving the poor from starvation would be just like taking too many people into a crowded lifeboat?

9 *Strength of support of reasons for conclusion*
The analogy is misleading. It is possible that the 'poor' could be saved from starvation without the 'rich' being dragged down to starvation level. Even if the analogy were convincing, to the extent that not everyone could be saved, it does not follow that those who are now poor should be the ones who are left to starve.

Passage 7

1 *Conclusion*
Although there appears to be no explicitly stated conclusion, the passage aims to get us to accept that we should be concerned about the survival of endangered species.

2 *Reasons and assumptions*

Four reasons are given:

Reason 1:

> other creatures have a basic right in themselves to be treated as equally valuable expressions of evolution as we humans

Reason 2:

> our own self-interest may depend on some future use we come to make of these species or the habitats on which they depend

Reason 3:

> we have no right to deprive future generations of their enjoyment or use of these creatures

Reason 4:

> more important than all of these is the fact that we owe it to ourselves, right here and now, to fulfil our obligation to act as stewards of the heaving and mysterious multitude of life.

The four reasons can be seen as jointly providing a justification for trying to ensure the survival of endangered species.

There is an assumption that we ought to think about the welfare of future generations.

3 *Truth of reasons and assumptions*
Reasons 1 and 4 are difficult to assess for truth, since they depend upon ideas about rights and obligations, without fully spelling out why we should think that these rights and obligations exist. Reason 2 can be accepted, because it simply says that it *may* turn out to be in our interests to ensure survival of endangered species. Reason 3, and its related assumption seem reasonable – we should surely have some concern about the welfare of future generations of human beings.

4 *Reliability of authorities*
The passage does not mention any authorities.

5 *Additional evidence*

It is difficult to think of additional evidence which may count against the conclusion, because the conclusion is not making a strong recommendation to act in a particular way.

6 *Drawing conclusions*

There are no obvious further conclusions to be drawn from the information given.

7 *Explanations*

No explanations of evidence are offered.

8 *Analogies*

There are no analogies or comparisons.

9 *Strength of support of reasons for conclusion*

It is difficult to assess the extent to which the conclusion is supported, without a deeper analysis of the idea of the rights of other creatures, and the obligations of humans as stewards. You may wish to think about this argument again when you have worked through Chapter 5, and also when you have thought about the section on Ethics and the Environment in Appendix 2. If the argument were making a strong recommendation that we should make every attempt possible to save endangered species, then we should want to assess the costs of these efforts, as well as the benefits suggested by Reasons 2 and 3.

Passage 9

1 *Conclusion*

The argument concludes that now is the time for Britain to do as the Americans do, and forbid religious worship and teaching in state schools.

2 *Reasons and assumptions*

The reasoning can be construed as follows:

Reason 1:

there is no satisfactory legal definition of a religion

Reason 2:

A religion is just a cult with more followers

These two reasons are offered jointly to support an intermediate conclusion that:

> once some are allowed sectarian education, there is no reason why others shouldn't be allowed their schools too – New Agers, astrologists, Moonies or any other sect or cult with a sufficient number of followers.

There is an assumption that allowing religious worship and teaching in state schools could prompt various sects and cults to set up their own schools, and an assumption that it would be a bad thing if cults were allowed to set up their own schools.

3 *Truth of reasons and assumptions*
It is not clear whether Reasons 1 and 2 are true – perhaps there could be a definition of a religion which could rule out the cults mentioned. The assumption that cults might want to set up their own schools does not seem to be borne out by experience.

4 *Reliability of authorities*
The passage does not mention any authorities.

5 *Additional evidence*
We could point out that special schools for cults of the kind the author mentions have not been proposed, despite the fact that religion is taught in schools, and special schools for religions such as Catholicism exist.

6 *Drawing conclusions*
There are no obvious further conclusions to be drawn from the information given.

7 *Explanations*
No explanations of evidence are offered.

8 *Analogies*
There is an implicit comparison between religions and cults.

9 *Strength of support of reasons for conclusion*
The conclusion has been argued for by suggesting that there are undesirable implications of allowing religious worship or teaching in schools. But the implications are simply that certain cults (which may be thought to be promoting mistaken ideas) could easily claim entitlement to set up

their own schools. No evidence is produced that this danger is about to be realised, or that it could not be dealt with under present laws, so the case for legislation is not very strong.

Appendix 2 – Summaries on specific ethical issues

Abortion

The two most extreme views on abortion are:

(i) abortion in any circumstances is morally wrong,
(ii) there is nothing morally wrong with abortion.

These views are often defended with claims about rights.

Rights of foetuses?

Anti-abortionists may claim that abortion is wrong because the foetus has a right to life.

Some justifications for thinking the foetus has a right to life
(a) *The foetus is a human being.*
The foetus certainly is human as opposed to being, for instance, feline, canine, or a piece of inorganic matter. But does that mean that it is already a member of the human moral community, such that it has the kind of entitlements which fully fledged persons have?

(b) *The foetus is a potential person.*

One view is that because the foetus has the potential for developing into an adult human being, we should treat it in the same way as we treat other persons. Two problems with this view have been pointed out:

(i) The fact that something has the potential to become *x* is not a good reason for treating it now as if it were *x*. (See Harris 1991: 11.)

(ii) Each sperm and each egg has the potential for developing, given the right conditions, so if potential is what matters, we shouldn't prevent those conditions from occurring, i.e. shouldn't use contraception. (See Harris 1991:12.)

What is claimed to be the relevant difference between sperm and eggs on the one hand and the fertilised egg on the other is that the fertilised egg has the full genetic endowment for becoming a human being – once fertilised it has the potential in itself.

So perhaps (ii) is not so strong an objection as (i).

(c) *The foetus is already a person.*

If so, at what stage did it become one, since anti-abortionists claim that abortion is impermissible after that time?

(i) Conception?

At this stage it is very different from us – it doesn't yet have the beginnings of development of the brain and central nervous system, so it can't feel pain, think, have emotions.

(ii) Viability?

(i.e. when the foetus could survive independently of mother, as babies prematurely born can.) But whether or not it can survive is dependent upon the state of medical technology. So a premature baby born today which survives might not have survived if it had been born 100 years ago. That would make its rights dependent upon when it happened to be born, but shouldn't rights be dependent upon inherent features of an entity?

(iii) Birth?

If the foetus doesn't become a person until birth, then abortion is permissible at any time during pregnancy. But what are the essential differences between a baby just before its birth and just after it which could guarantee that it was a person immediately after birth but not before?

It seems very difficult to find a sharp dividing line before which the foetus is not a person, and after which it is.

The concept of a person

(See our discussion of the concept of a person in Chapter 4, and Harris 1991, Chapter 1.)

The argument that the foetus is not a person goes as follows. Anything which is not self-conscious is not a person. Self-consciousness is not possible unless one can be aware of oneself as one among others, hence aware that there are other centres of consciousness. The perception of other centres of consciousness is possible only for beings which communicate. The foetus cannot communicate with others. So the foetus is not a person.

There is a problem for this view, which is that not only is the foetus not aware of other centres of consciousness, it is probable that neither is the new-born baby. So if only persons have a right to life, and new born babies are no more persons than foetuses are, this licenses infanticide as well as abortion, unless there are some other reasons why infanticide is wrong – perhaps because it has undesirable consequences which abortion does not have, e.g. making us less inclined to respect the right to life where it should be respected. (See Tooley (1986) for a discussion on abortion and infanticide.)

Rights of mothers?

Those who are not against abortion might rely on one of two assumptions:

(i)   The foetus has rights, but these are of lesser importance than the mother's rights.
(ii) The foetus has no rights.

Suppose the foetus has rights

If the foetus has a right to life, what rights *could* the mother have which would override *this*?

(a)   *Mother's right to protect her own life*
There are rare cases where an abortion would be necessary in order to save the life of the mother. How can we choose between them if they have an equal right to life?
Some people may rely on the distinction between killing and letting die. Abortion involves killing the foetus; doing nothing is a matter of letting the mother die. If killing is always morally worse than letting die, abortion is not

permissible in these cases. (See Chapter 5 for a discussion of the doctrine of acts and omissions.)

In Exercise 4 you assessed an extract from J.J. Thomson 'A Defense of Abortion'. You will remember that she tells a story: You wake up one morning to find that a kidney patient has been attached to your kidneys. If you stay thus attached then in nine months he will be cured of his fatal disease, and able to survive independently. But he will die if you detach yourself before then, because, until he is cured, he needs to be attached to someone else's kidneys, and you alone have the right blood group to help. Suppose this person (the violinist) were to be saved at the expense of your life – you remain attached to him for nine months, then you die and he survives, or you detach yourself, you survive and he dies. This is supposed to parallel the case of the mother whose life is threatened by a pregnancy. Thomson argues that the mother who aborts the foetus would be acting in self-defence, saving her life because it was threatened by someone else – and that even though the foetus has a right to life, it is not wrong for the mother to kill it in order to save her own life.

There are two problems for this.

(i)   Usually when we condone killing in self-defence, it is in cases where the person threatening someone's life is doing so deliberately – or at least is doing something which they should be able to see is putting someone else's life in danger. But the foetus is neither deliberately threatening mother's life, nor able to see that its existence threatens mother's life.

(ii)   The person attached to the violinist seems to have no responsibility for him. Does the mother have a responsibility for the foetus?

(b)   *Woman's right over what happens to her body*
One view is that rather than the right to life (of the foetus) having priority, the mother's right to determine what happens to her own body has priority.

Why? Because the right to life does not require that others do absolutely anything to save us, and does not require that others give us the use of their body in order to save us. (An implication of this position is that it *can* distinguish morally between abortion and infanticide – because apart from imaginary examples like the violinist, abortion is claimed to be the only case of killing which involves exercising the right to control over one's own body. So there are no implications for the permissibility of killing in general or the permissibility of infanticide.)

According to Thomson, if you could save the violinist not by dying yourself, but simply by letting him use your kidneys for nine months, you have no duty to do that, and he doesn't have the right to the use of your kidneys. Thomson seems to suggest that this is because *you* gave him no right to use your kidneys, and this seems to be based on the general principle that one can have a right to the use of someone else's body only if the person in question gave one that right.

To apply that to the case of the foetus, in what circumstances has a foetus been given the right to use the mother's body? Has the mother given the right to the foetus just by being pregnant? Perhaps not if pregnancy is the result of rape, or the mother has attempted not to conceive. But suppose pregnancy results from intercourse to which mother has consented, and she has not taken precautions against conception. Has she implicitly given the foetus the right to the use of her body? If so, and if the foetus is a person (at whatever stage), and if persons have a right to life, then abortion at the stage at which the foetus becomes a person must be wrong.

In assessing arguments based on the woman's right to control over her own body, we need to think about:

What exactly does the right to life involve? Does it require others to take positive steps to preserve our lives (e.g. saving someone who is drowning, giving food to the starving, administering drugs, operating on someone)?

Is the only way in which the foetus could acquire a right to the use of its mother's body by being given that right by her?

Suppose the foetus has no rights

We still have to consider harm that could be done to a foetus, even if it has no rights. The most obvious way in which it could possibly be harmed by an abortion is in suffering pain.

(a) *Is the foetus capable of suffering pain?*
It is not capable of suffering pain until its nervous system is sufficiently developed, but it is not absolutely clear when this is. The most recent claim by scientists, in a report from the Royal College of Obstetricians and Gynaecologists in October 1997, is that the foetus cannot feel pain before 26 weeks into the pregnancy.

(b) *Is the foetus's capacity for suffering pain relevant?*
Could the foetus be anaesthetised against pain during abortion? A report in the *Independent* of 25 October 1997 quotes Ann Furedi of the pro-choice charity, the Birth Control Trust, as saying that 'In abortions at and after 20 weeks, the foetal heart is always stopped prior to the abortion so there is already no possibility that the foetus could suffer'.

(c) *Consideration of the consequences*

If the foetus has no right to life, and if we can ensure that the foetus will not suffer pain during an abortion, is it morally acceptable for a woman to have an abortion at any stage of pregnancy, for any reason whatsoever?

Should we also consider the consequences of an individual's decision to have an abortion, e.g. who else is affected, both favourably and adversely?

Should we consider the consequences of legislation on abortion – for medical staff, and for the general population?

It might be claimed that if infanticide were not illegal, there would be a danger of callousness towards babies, even after they had become persons. Would late abortions have similar adverse effects? Would this be a way of making a distinction between abortion and infanticide, such that abortion is morally permissible and infanticide is not, even if neither foetus nor neonate has a right to life?

Is the concept of rights helpful?

You need to consider whether the concept of rights is helpful in settling questions about abortion. The debate is usually conducted in these terms, but it could be expressed instead in terms of the wrongness of killing. Dworkin (1993), Norman (1995) and Hursthouse (1987) offer interesting perspectives on the issue.

Further reading

Dworkin, R. (1993) *Life's Dominion*, London: Harper-Collins.

Glover, J. (1990) *Causing Death and Saving Lives*, London: Penguin, chapters 9, 10 and 11.

Harris J. (1991) *The Value of Life*, London: Routledge & Kegan Paul, chapters 1 and 8.

Hursthouse, R. (1987) *Beginning Lives*, Oxford: Blackwell.

Norman, R. (1995) *Ethics, Killing and War*, Cambridge: Cambridge University Press, chapter 2.

Singer, P. (1993) *Practical Ethics*, 2nd edn, Cambridge: Cambridge University Press, chapter 6.

Thomson, J.J. (1986) 'A Defense of Abortion', in P. Singer (ed.) *Applied Ethics*, Oxford: Oxford University Press.

Tooley, M. (1986) 'Abortion and Infanticide', in P. Singer (ed.) *Applied Ethics*, Oxford: Oxford University Press.

Euthanasia

Definition and distinctions

Definition

> Euthanasia = bringing about someone's death because to do so would be in that person's interests.

Active/passive distinction

Active – performing an action which causes death, e.g. giving a lethal injection

Passive – not taking steps to prolong life, e.g. not putting on life support machine, not treating pneumonia in the elderly, not feeding malformed babies.

Voluntary/involuntary/non-voluntary distinctions

Voluntary = patients request that their death be brought about because life is not worth living, perhaps in circumstances in which it is impossible for them to commit suicide, or perhaps because they want their death to be in expert hands, so that it can be quick and painless.

Involuntary = the patient has expressed a wish to go on living (or has not been consulted about it), but it is judged to be in the patient's interest to die. Most writers on the subject simply take it for granted that it is always wrong to take someone's life when they have expressed the wish to go on living, but it might be less easy to justify the claim that you should never let someone die who has expressed the wish to go on living. Think about whether, for example, it would be wrong to fail to resuscitate someone with a painful terminal illness whose heart stops, but who has said they want to be resuscitated if this should happen to them.

Non-voluntary = the patient is incapable of having a preference, or incapable of expressing a preference for death over life (e.g. due to brain damage).

Is the active/passive distinction morally relevant?

The distinction relies on the doctrine of acts and omissions to the effect that:

> There is a moral difference between *performing an act* which has certain consequences, and *failing to act* when that failure to act has exactly the same consequences.

We discussed this doctrine in Chapter 5. For further discussion of it, in particular as it relates to euthanasia, see Rachels (1986) and Foot (1977). Rachels argues that there is no intrinsic moral difference between active and passive euthanasia, though there may be moral differences due to their consequences. Foot claims that there is an essential moral difference between active and passive euthanasia. She claims that this is because the right to life is a right not to be killed, but does not include a right to be kept alive, especially if 'abnormal means' are necessary to keep one alive. Is this distinction between normal and abnormal means of keeping people alive appropriate? Can it settle particular cases? For example, is a heart transplant a normal means?

Is voluntary euthanasia morally permissible?

If a patient requests euthanasia, and it would be in that patient's interest that their life should end, then euthanasia would not infringe the right to life, or the requirement to respect autonomy. So if voluntary euthanasia is morally wrong, that must be either because it is wrong to kill a person even if that person wishes to die, or because it would have consequences which were worse than the killing, or because it would infringe someone else's rights, (though some might argue that people have a right to die as they wish, regardless of consequences for others).

Some problems for deciding whether a particular case of voluntary euthanasia is morally right:

(i)   can we be sure the person's expressed wish is genuine?
(ii) can we be sure that death is in the person's interest?
(iii) can we judge what bad side effects there might be?

Is non-voluntary euthanasia morally wrong?

A decision about non-voluntary euthanasia could be required in two kinds of cases:

1 Those who have been capable of making their own decisions, but are now incapable, e.g. those in a Permanent Vegetative State (PVS), or those on a life-support system.

   If such individuals did not satisfy the criteria for being a person, and if only persons have a right to life, then bringing about their deaths would not be an infringement of the right to life. Can we be certain that if there is no detectable higher brain activity in such cases, then there is no awareness of what is happening, and no self-consciousness?

Perhaps we cannot distinguish between those who are incapable of having a preference, and those who are merely incapable of expressing their preferences. One category of patients – the elderly with senile dementia – may have preferences which they cannot tell us about. No-one suggests that such people should be killed when others judge that their quality of life is very poor. One reason why killing is thought to be wrong in such cases is that it would be likely to lead to fearfulness amongst the population. Yet these patients are often allowed to die, when, for example, they get pneumonia which could be treated with antibiotics. Is the distinction between killing and letting die morally relevant in these cases?

It is sometimes suggested that 'living wills' should be made legally binding. These would allow each of us to express our wishes as to how we should be treated if we were to be in the position of PVS, life-support or senile dementia patients. Would this be a good way of enabling others to make decisions about euthanasia in such cases?

2 Those who have never been capable of making their own decisions (e.g. infants).

If killing is wrong principally because it ends the life of a self-conscious being, and if infants are not self-conscious, then killing infants is not intrinsically wrong (see our discussion of the concept of a person in Chapter 4 and in the section on abortion).

Peter Singer suggests that the moral difference between killing a severely disabled and a non-disabled infant is due to the effects on others (principally the parents), and also to judgements about the quality of life which could be expected for the child. He describes severe cases of spina bifida in which it is often judged that the child's life would involve unbearable suffering (Singer 1993: 184). In some cases of disability, it will be difficult to make judgements about quality of life.

Singer mentions the 'replaceability' criterion – the view that it is not wrong to end one life if we can replace it with a life of better quality. This is an implication of classical utilitarianism, which aims at producing the highest possible level of happiness in the world. Although he does not believe that we should accept 'replaceability' for self-conscious beings, he thinks we should in relation to disabled infants. He justifies this by saying that we accept it in relation to abortion when severe foetal abnormalities are taken to be good reason for parents to choose abortion and subsequently try to produce a non-disabled child. Why should we not accept it in relation to infanticide, if the foetus and the infant have the same moral status?

Is it wrong to bring about someone's death as a side-effect?

We discussed the doctrine of double effect in Chapter 5. It says:

One need not be held responsible for those effects of one's actions, which, though foreseen, are not intended, provided that:

(i) the action performed is done because it will have some good effect, even though it may also have bad effects, and
(ii) one intends only the good effects and not the bad effects of the action.
(iii) the bad effect is not the means by which the good effect is achieved.

You will remember that the article by Melanie Phillips in Exercise 4 suggested that it is morally acceptable to 'administer pain relief which might have the side-effect of hastening the death of an already dying patient', although she was opposed to voluntary euthanasia.

The chief objections to the doctrine are that only the outcome matters, so intentions are irrelevant (a utilitarian objection); or that one must be held responsible for the results of one's action which one *knows* will occur.

Rejecting the doctrine implies that there is no intrinsic moral difference between administering the injection which hastens death and giving an injection which causes death, but contains no painkiller. This means that if administering the painkiller is right, then giving the fatal injection is right, and if giving the fatal injection is wrong, then administering the painkiller is wrong, unless there are differences between the two in terms of their consequences.

The idea that it is not wrong to bring about someone's death as a side-effect of administering pain killing drugs was given legal backing in a court case in October 1997. This concerned Annie Lindsell, who was the subject of one of your decision-making tasks in Exercise 5. Although there was no formal legal judgement on the case, medical experts at the court confirmed that it was permissible to relieve pain for terminally ill patients, even if it shortened their lives. Ms Lindsell's doctor then agreed that he would give diamorphine if Ms Lindsell requested it. It was reported on 3 December 1997 that she had died without it having been necessary to administer the drug.

Should voluntary euthanasia be legalised?

Voluntary euthanasia does not infringe rights or the requirement to respect autonomy. Some people may insist, usually because of religious views, that it is wrong because life is sacred.

If it is not wrong, why should it not be legalised? Some possible reasons concern consequences of legalising it, and you will have to consider whether these outweigh the harm to and autonomy of patients.

Some possible bad consequences are:

(i)   fears of patients going into hospital,
(ii) pressure on the elderly to volunteer,
(iii) even without pressure, guilt of the elderly who don't opt for it,
(iv) it may make it less likely that good terminal care would be provided
(v)   there may be abuse of the law such that involuntary euthanasia occurs.

We need to consider also a possible good consequence of legalising euthanasia, which is that it would remove the burden of decision from doctors.

Further reading

Beauchamp, T.L. and Childress, J.F. (1983) *Principles of Biomedical Ethics*, New York and Oxford: Oxford University Press.

Campbell, R. and Collinson, D. (1988) *Ending Lives*, Oxford: Blackwell.

Foot, P. (1977) 'Euthanasia', *Philosophy and Public Affairs*, vol. 6, no. 2.

Glover, J. (1977) *Causing Death and Saving Lives*, London: Penguin, chapters 14 and 15.

Harris J. (1985) *The Value of Life*, London: Routledge & Kegan Paul, chapters 2, 3 and 4.

Rachels, J. (1986) 'Active and Passive Euthanasia', in P. Singer (ed.) *Applied Ethics*, Oxford: Oxford University Press.

Singer, P. (1993) *Practical Ethics*, 2nd edn, Cambridge: Cambridge University Press, chapter 7.

Ethics and animals

Humans kill other animals for meat, sport, furs and skins. They kill animals regarded as pests, animals which are injured or very ill, and animals which, it is claimed, need to be 'culled'. They cause pain and distress to animals in the process of meat production, through factory farming and methods of slaughter. They use animals in scientific experiments for the benefit of humans, and they keep animals confined in zoos.

You need to consider to what extent the following two principles apply to animals:

It is wrong to cause pain and distress.

It is wrong to kill.

The welfare of animals is often discussed as an issue of 'animal rights'. Can we settle ethical questions about animals without referring to the concept of animal rights? Is it appropriate to talk about rights at all in relation to animals?

Is it wrong to cause pain and distress to animals?

If we accept as a basic moral principle that we should not cause avoidable harm, then we must accept that we should not cause avoidable harm to animals. The suffering of animals is just as much something to be avoided as is the suffering of humans. It is clear that pain and fear are harmful to animals, so we shouldn't be inflicting it.

What are the practical implications of accepting that we should not cause suffering to animals? Should we all be vegetarians if we know that animals are not well treated in the process of meat production? Should we campaign against factory farming, hunting and the use of animals in experiments? What about zoos? Do animals kept in captivity suffer?

Utilitarian view on animal suffering

If the aim is for the well-being of the greatest number, then this must be the greatest number of whatever is capable of experiencing happiness, pleasure, pain or distress. Sometimes a gain in the general happiness may outweigh suffering. The utilitarian can say that it's acceptable to inflict pain for the sake of an increase in the general happiness, even when the one who suffers pain is not going to share the general happiness. So it could be acceptable to utilitarians to experiment on animals if this suffering would be outweighed by a great increase in general happiness.

Strictly speaking, under utilitarianism, the suffering of a human being may be justified – yet we are very unlikely to find utilitarians advocating experimenting on humans for the general good (unless of course, they are volunteers, e.g. drug trials).

Why not? The rationale would be that it would lead to great unhappiness if people knew that such experiments took place. But, since animals couldn't have knowledge that animal experiments occurred, then it may be justifiable to do experiments which caused suffering to animals (only, of course, if there were no less harmful way of doing the research).

Is it wrong to kill animals?

It is often claimed that it is wrong to kill animals, because just as humans have rights, so do animals.

Humans could survive without killing animals, so if animals have a right to life, one cannot see what excuses we could have for killing them. What arguments could be used to claim that animals have a right to life?

Speciesism

In Exercises 6 and 7 you thought about the concept of 'speciesism', a term used by Peter Singer. Singer himself does not claim that animals have rights, but the idea of speciesism may be used by others to defend the idea of animal rights.

Suppose someone claims that the mere fact that all humans are members of our species, and all animals are not, implies that humans have greater worth or value. This would be 'speciesism' – and Singer calls it that because he thinks it is analogous to racism and sexism. Denying someone certain rights *just because* they are a member of a particular race, or just because they are male or female, is considered to be unjust. But denying rights to animals *just because* they are not humans would be exactly like this. And if racism and sexism are wrong, then speciesism must be wrong also.

In some places, Singer (*Animal Liberation* 1973) defines speciesism as 'a prejudice or attitude of bias towards the interests of members of one's own species and against those of other species'. If that is what speciesism is, then of course it is a bad thing, because it has been defined as a prejudice, and a prejudice is a belief or attitude which we hold for no good reason. But if speciesism is defined more neutrally as 'the belief that members of different species have different moral status or significance', then it will only be a bad thing if there are no morally significant differences between species, i.e. if the differing characteristics of species have no bearing at all on how we should treat them. So what we have to ask in relation to speciesism is, are any of the differences between species morally significant?

What does the idea of speciesism imply about whether it is wrong to kill animals? Singer thinks there should be 'equality of consideration' for animals as well as for humans. This does not depend on any claim that we are all equal (since, in many ways we are not), nor does it imply that everyone should have exactly the same rights. But it does mean that you can't deny animals rights just because they are animals.

Does this establish that animals have a right to life, or that if we shouldn't kill humans, then we shouldn't kill animals? Singer acknowledges that 'equality of consideration' doesn't imply exactly the same treatment, and exactly the same rights for all beings. So again, we have to ask, are there any differences between humans and animals in virtue of which humans possess a right to life whereas animals do not?

Consciousness

If this were the criterion of having rights, then surely some animals would have rights, since we are in little doubt that some animals experience pain, pleasure, emotions.

Self-consciousness

This criterion appeared in relation to our analysis of the concept of a person in Chapter 5. The reason for relying on self-consciousness rather than simply consciousness is the idea that the life of a being which can value its own life must have greater value. The criterion is: awareness of oneself as an entity existing over time, including awareness of one's past and one's future. Some animals may have this characteristic. Many probably do not.

Singer, despite his views on speciesism, *does* accept that the life of a self-conscious being has more worth than the life of a non-self-conscious being. So he would have to accept that the killing of animals which were not self-conscious was less bad, morally, than the killing of animals which were self-conscious. The dispute then becomes one, not about whether the characteristic of self-consciousness is morally relevant to the questions about rights to life, but about which animals have this characteristic.

One problem for anyone using this characteristic to exclude some animals from the right to life is that some humans may not have the characteristic either, e.g. those who are severely mentally handicapped. So if it means animals can't have rights, does it mean that some humans can't either?

One way to defend the idea that it doesn't is to say that humans who don't have the characteristic of self-consciousness are to be counted as persons because, simply by being human, they might have been persons, but by misfortune they are not – and that a misfortune shouldn't be the ground for excluding someone from full moral status.

Animals cannot be members of a moral community

This was Polly Toynbee's position in the extract in Exercise 6. The idea behind it is that morality is a social contract. This assumes that every rational being seeks to maximise its own interest, and so will accept a morality (which necessarily imposes some restrictions) only if this morality is of benefit to the individual. A rational being will see that it is rational to put oneself under commitments to other rational beings, who similarly agree to be bound by moral rules. In that way each person will do better than they would have done if there were no rules, because all others will be conceding rights to them. However, animals will not be able to understand the basis of a social contract, and will not be able to respect the rights of others, so it will scarcely be possible, and certainly not rational to enter into a social contract with animals. So if a social contract deriving from egoism is the source of rights then animals cannot have rights.

Sometimes a similar point is made without talking about morality being based on egoism. It might be said that having a right is conditional upon being able to respect the rights of others, i.e. that those who have rights also have duties to respect the rights of others. It is then claimed that animals can't have duties, because they would not be able to understand and operate with the concept of a duty, so they can't have rights either.

This point about animals not being able to operate with the concept of a duty is closely tied up with the idea of self-consciousness. In order to operate with the concept of a duty, you must be able to see yourself as someone who has obligations which you might be tempted not to fulfil.

A negative or a positive right?

If animals have a right to life, does it imply merely that we shouldn't kill them, or does it imply also that we should attempt to keep animals alive? If it were a positive right, it would have implications for medical treatment of animals, and for attempts to ensure that wild animals do not die.

Utilitarian view on killing animals

It would probably be bad for the general well-being if people's lives were not highly valued, because people can worry about their own futures. They make plans for the future, and want to believe that those plans will be realised. If they knew that life was not highly valued, this would make everyone feel insecure, so it wouldn't be a good thing.

But if animals can't worry about the future, then they could not know that animals' lives were not highly valued, and couldn't feel insecure in the same way. This is why utilitarians such as Singer concede that it *is* less serious to take the life of an animal than to take the life of a human being.

Remember that killing is not intrinsically wrong under utilitarianism, i.e. if it is wrong, that cannot simply be because it is a case of killing. Its rightness or wrongness must depend upon:

(i) the effects on others (making them directly unhappy because someone they care about has died, or making them insecure)
(ii) pleasure or happiness which would have been experienced by one who dies. This is the case with animals as well as humans.

The effects on other animals of the deaths of animals may not be as severe as the effects on other humans of the deaths of humans.

What about the second criterion – the happiness which would have been experienced by the one who dies?

Problems with using this as a criterion:

(i)   Difficulties in making the calculation. Should we think of animals' pleasure or suffering being just the same as humans'? Does that depend on what species of animal it is?

(ii) To rely on this criterion is to concede that happiness which could have been experienced if someone had been alive is relevant to the question as to whether an action is wrong. But this is parallel to the happiness which would have been experienced by all the children we could have brought into the world, but haven't. So if unrealised happiness makes killing wrong, then it also makes failure to conceive wrong. But surely, failure to conceive cannot be wrong. So how can it be true that it is the fact of happiness which would otherwise have been experienced which makes killing wrong?

(iii) A related problem. If killing is wrong on the grounds that it deprives the world of a happy life, then should we say that it is acceptable to kill provided one replaces the life which is lost with another one which is equally happy?

On these two points, (the wrongness of non-conception, and the replaceability of animals/persons), Singer distinguishes between two versions of utilitarianism:

(i)   *The prior existence version*
In making the moral decision, we take into account only those beings already in existence. In relation to killing, for example, we consider whether killing the person/animal will lead to an increase or a decrease in pleasure for those beings now in existence.

(ii) *The total version*
It is good to increase the total amount of pleasure in the world (and reduce the total amount of pain). It doesn't matter whether this is done by increasing the pleasure of existing beings or increasing the number of beings who exist.

It is the total version which leads to the problems in (b) and (c). If it is morally acceptable to think of animals as replaceable, then it would be morally acceptable to kill animals for meat, because you can replace one life with another. It might even be suggested that if we didn't raise and kill animals for meat, there would be fewer animals around, and therefore less pleasure in the world. However, the objection to that is that if we didn't raise animals for meat, we could grow more crops, and thus be able to feed more humans who could have happy lives.

What view does Singer favour? For self-conscious beings, the prior existence view – thus for self-conscious beings we must not regard them as replaceable. For non-self-conscious beings, the total view – thus we can regard them as replaceable. Singer thinks that many animals are self-conscious, but perhaps fish are not self-conscious.

Further reading

Clarke, S. (1984) *The Moral Status of Animals*, Oxford: Clarendon Press.
LaFollette, H. and Shanks, N. (1996) *Brute Science*, London and New York: Routledge.
Midgley, M. (1983) *Animals and Why They Matter*, Harmondsworth: Penguin.
Regan, T. and Singer, P. (1976) *Animal Rights and Human Obligations*, Englewood Cliffs and London: Prentice Hall.
Singer, P. (1993) *Practical Ethics*, 2nd edn, Cambridge: Cambridge University Press, chapter 5.
—— (1986b) All Animals are Equal', in P. Singer (ed.) *Applied Ethics*, Oxford: Oxford University Press.

Ethics and the environment

What is the basis for environmental ethics?

Anthropocentrism

We should protect the environment in so far as to do so would protect the interests of human beings. This may be a claim about the usefulness to humans of aspects of the physical world, and/or about the aesthetic value of nature – the pleasure which it gives to humans. It is a view which holds that animals, plants and the non-living physical world have no moral status, except indirectly because of their relationship with human beings.

Interests of sentient beings

We should not engage in activities which have adverse effects on sentient beings, present and future. 'Sentient' means having the capacity for experiencing pain and pleasure, having wants and desires which could be satisfied or thwarted. This includes animals as well as human beings.

We should have respect for anything which is living, hence plants are included also. This view is associated with Albert Schweitzer, who believed that all forms of life are equally valuable.

Two problems with this view:

(i) Plants do not have wants and desires, therefore cannot be said to have interests. Singer says that talking about the interests of plants is 'merely metaphorical'.

(ii) Since we have to eat in order to live, and since our food comes from living things, then we have to exploit living things in order to survive. Does the idea of reverence for life imply that it is just as bad to pick and eat an apple as it is to kill a human being? Perhaps not, since eating the apple doesn't require killing the apple tree. So perhaps you *can* hold that all forms of life are equally valuable, and still believe that so long as we keep to a vegetarian diet, we are not doing anything wrong.

Even so, we might sometimes be faced with having to choose between the survival of two different forms of life, where the survival of both isn't possible, e.g. if a colony of rats which carry disease is threatening to wipe out a human population, we might choose to save the human population by killing the rats. But if all forms of life are equally valuable, then we have as much reason to leave the rats alone and let the human beings die.

You may remember the passage by Nicholas Schoon in Exercise 4, in which he claimed that although every species is of equal value, nevertheless human beings have the right to destroy other species which cause serious suffering and death to people. Look back at his reasons for this claim, and judge whether they are good reasons for his conclusion.

Deep ecology and the land ethic

Everything is morally relevant. It is not just that which is human, conscious or alive that matters. Everything in the world has value in its own right. At first sight this might appear to be a claim that each individual thing in the world has intrinsic value, in common with the previous positions, but extending the list of individual things to include, for example, rocks, lakes, beaches, and so on. But the view is rather that the system as a whole has value, and deep ecologists may have less in common with people concerned about animal welfare than we would imagine. The view can be summarised in the following quotation from Aldo Leopold (1966): 'A thing is right when it tends to preserve the integrity, stability and beauty of the biotic community. It is wrong when it tends otherwise'. Leopold himself was in favour of hunting and killing wild animals, so his view was different from that of animal welfarists.

Differences between Leopold and animal welfarists such as Singer are as follows:

(i) A different conception of the nature of the world
Seeing the world as a unified system, an organic whole, NOT simply as a collection of objects, some of which are alive and some of which are conscious. The world is viewed as a system which has value in itself (intrinsic value).

(ii) A different basis for justifying actions:
Instead of asking 'what pain or pleasure will our actions cause or what interests will they satisfy or thwart?', we should ask 'what is the effect of our actions on the ecological system?'

(iii) Leads to different recommendations
There may be agreement on issues such as pollution, destruction of habitats for human convenience etc, since it may be true that such activities are both harmful to individuals and destructive of the integrity and stability of the ecosphere.

But what about issues arising from competition between species? Deep ecologists think we should intervene in the natural world when order and stability are threatened in some way. Some examples of current or recent disputes in which deep ecologists would make different recommendations from those who campaign for animal welfare:

(i) In recent years the Royal Society for the Protection of Birds has taken steps to control the numbers of ruddy duck, a species which was originally introduced to Britain from North America, and whose numbers threaten the survival of indigenous species by monopolising food supplies. The Society was criticised by animal welfarists.

(ii) For similar reasons, grey squirrels may be killed in order to safeguard red squirrels. Animal welfarists may be opposed to this.

(iii) Elephant culling – in Zimbabwe's Hwange National Park, it is proposed that, contrary to the wishes of many animal welfarists, many thousands of elephants be shot over the next few years, in order to protect the park habitat from the impact of the increasing elephant population.

Problems for applying the deep ecologists' view

(i)   How do we judge that nature is in balance? What counts as 'integrity, stability and beauty of the biosphere'?

'Beauty' seems to be a characteristic which something could have only in relation to beings who regarded it as beautiful, and yet these characteristics are supposed to be intrinsic, independent of the value the biosphere has for humans.

How do we know when integrity and stability are achieved? Is it better if there are a million and one species in the world than if there are a million?

(ii)   Why should the fact that there *is* a balance of nature tell us anything about what *ought* to be the case?

Is the fact that something is natural a good reason for preserving it?

Duties to future generations, human and animal

Suppose we reject the idea that nature has intrinsic value, and we base our ideas about how we should protect the environment on the value of the environment to sentient beings. Should we take account of future generations? What demands can future generations reasonably be said to impose on us?

Problems for a utilitarian position

Will there be more happiness if, for example, we leave non-renewable resources such as oil for future generations to use? The difficulties for utilitarianism are difficulties about establishing facts about, for example, which generation will get the most benefit from oil. Since we cannot be absolutely certain about the answer to that, perhaps it doesn't much matter which generation uses it.

In relation to pollution, we might have to sacrifice some of our pleasurable activities now in order to ensure greater happiness for others in the future. Remember that utilitarianism requires us to consider the welfare of not only those we know, but of the whole population of the world, and of all possible future generations.

Problems for rights theorists

It seems strange to talk about the rights of people, or animals, who don't yet exist, so perhaps an ethical approach based on rights is not appropriate in environmental ethics.

Despite these problems, both for utilitarianism and for rights theories, the idea of our duties to future generations does not seem totally absurd. If we believe that there will be people living on earth in 200 years time, it seems unfair that we should consider only our own comfort and welfare now.

Further reading

Attfield, R. (1983) *The Ethics of Environmental Concern*, Oxford: Blackwell.
Leopold, A. (1966) *A Sand County Almanac*, New York: Oxford University Press.
Singer, P. (1993) *Practical Ethics*, 2nd edn, Cambridge: Cambridge University Press, chapter 10.

Capital punishment

Justifications for punishment

What justification could there be for using punishment at all, whether it is capital punishment or any other kind?

Consequentialist theories justify everything in terms of consequences, so they justify punishment by its consequences. Non-consequentialist theories focus mainly on the idea of retribution – i.e. requiring someone to pay the appropriate penalty for his or her crime. Consequentialists focus either on the deterrent effect – the way in which punishing one person deters others from committing the same kind of crime, or on the reformative effect of punishment – i.e. punishing someone in order to ensure that they will behave better in the future. Thus the three possible types of justification for punishment are retribution, deterrence, and reform.

In relation to capital punishment, reform cannot apply, so retribution and deterrence are the two main justifications.

Retributivist view on capital punishment

This relies on the *lex talionis* (law of retaliation) 'an eye for an eye and a tooth for a tooth'. It involves the claim that punishment rightly involves paying back the offenders by making them suffer in the way their victims suffered. Thus we are to punish the taking of life by taking the life of the person who has committed the crime. So capital punishment of murderers is required.

It is assumed that the person is responsible for the action – it would not be appropriate to punish those who didn't know what they were doing or couldn't help doing it.

Retribution involves the idea that punishment is an expression of the moral attitudes of the community. The execution of a murderer expresses a view about the seriousness of murder. However, this differs from a consequentialist view that executions will have the *effect* of making people believe that murder is a serious crime. The retributivist view maintains that murderers ought to be executed even if executing murderers does not make people regard murder as serious. A retributivist view is presented by Kant (1785) in *The Foundations of the Metaphysic of Morals*.

Objections

(i)   Why use the death penalty if it has no beneficial results, especially since it is such a drastic thing to do? Utilitarians would ask why we should increase the suffering in the world if we are not going to achieve anything by it? Of course this comment won't make retributivists change their minds, because they will just deny the claim that it is the effect of punishment which matters.

(ii)   If each execution is to be justified by the fact the person executed deserves it, you have to know that you are executing the right person. Perhaps the retributivist will say that we almost always get it right. However, there have been many cases of miscarriages of justice.

(iii)   The idea of retribution only shows us that we have a **right** to punish the person, not that we have a **duty** to do so. It implies merely that someone who has done something wrong to someone else, cannot complain of unfair treatment if that same thing is done to them. This shows us that we are entitled to execute murderers, not that we must execute them. It remains open to us to forgive them, or to punish them in some way which we think will be socially useful.

(iv)   Nor does the idea of retribution imply that the punishment we give to murderers must be the same as they have done to their victims. It certainly requires that the worst crime is given the worst punishment which we ever give, but it will be consistent with retributivism if we say that the murderer has deserved execution, and couldn't complain of injustice if that's what he or she got, but that nevertheless the most severe punishment which we mete out is life imprisonment, so murderers will get life imprisonment.

If the *lex talionis* is taken strictly, it requires that rapists should be raped and that torturers should be tortured. But we would regard these kinds of punishment as morally unacceptable, so we don't have to take the *lex talionis* strictly, in any context. This view is expressed in Reiman (1985), and in the extract from an article by Michael Dummett in Exercise 2.

Utilitarian view on capital punishment

For the utilitarian, what justifies punishment is the consequences of the punishment. Critics often point out that this would justify punishing people who had committed no crime, provided that punishing them had the effect of deterring others from committing crimes. The reply is that utilitarians would never condone that, because allowing such things to happen would not be conducive to the general happiness. Assuming that utilitarians would not punish the innocent, they must ask what is the most effective way of treating criminals, what will have the best results. The death penalty would not be ruled out in principle, (nor would it necessarily be confined to cases of murder) but if it were believed to have worse effects than other forms of punishment, then it would not be right to use the death penalty.

What good consequences might it have? It would certainly be a totally effective means of preventing the criminal from re-offending, but there might be other ways of preventing re-offending, and there might be some crimes where the likelihood of re-offending was very small (for example, killings motivated by jealousy). It might work as a deterrent, making others less likely to commit murder.

Utilitarians do not rely simply on counting up the numbers of lives saved by having the death penalty. They must take account of the awful nature of the penalty, and the effects it has on those who have to carry it out, and on the families of the murderers. They would also have to consider the possibility of execution of the innocent, and the insecurity which this leads to. Some claim it makes jurors less willing to convict, thereby perhaps making it less likely that the innocent would be executed, but also making it more likely that those who are guilty would not be punished at all.

Utilitarians need to know first and foremost what the deterrent effect of the death penalty is. Two kinds of argument are put forward about deterrence.

(i) *Statistical evidence*
We can compare murder rates before and after the abolition of capital punishment, and murder rates in different countries (or different states of USA), one of which has death penalty, whereas the other does not.

The results of these comparisons don't show a correlation between the absence of the death penalty and a higher murder rate, so they do not provide evidence that the death penalty deters murderers. Some would say that neither do they show that the death penalty does not deter murderers, so if they show neither one thing nor the other, we should rely on our intuitions.

(ii)   *Intuitions*

One argument, which you saw in Exercise 3, about the deterrent effect of the death penalty goes as follows:

> Reason 1: Those offered a choice between execution and life imprisonment, will choose life imprisonment.
>
> Therefore,
>
> Intermediate conclusion: They fear death more than they fear life imprisonment.
>
> And
>
> Reason 2: People are most deterred by what they most fear.
>
> Therefore,
>
> Main conclusion: The threat of the death penalty is more of a deterrent than the threat of life imprisonment.

Criticisms of the above argument

The following criticisms are offered by Reiman (1985).

From the fact that people fear death more than they fear life imprisonment, it does not follow that the death penalty will deter them *more*. The threat of life imprisonment might be awful enough to deter many potential murderers. (This challenges the move from reason 2 to the conclusion.)

Criminals are not deterred by risk of death from armed police. In the USA, there is already a substantial risk to criminals of being killed by police while committing a crime, but the crime rate is still high. (This challenges the truth of reason 2.)

Potential murderers may not believe they will be executed, since they may not be thinking rationally, or they may think they will not be caught. (This challenges the move from the reasons to the conclusion, by pointing out that it relies on the dubious assumption that potential murderers believe they will be executed.)

Torturing to death would be more feared than painless death, therefore in order to achieve maximum deterrence, we should torture murderers before we kill them. (Attempts to undermine the argument by showing that it has further implications, which may be regarded as unacceptable.)

Reasons for opposing capital punishment

(i)   The absolutist view –capital punishment violates the right to life

The absolutist position says that capital punishment is wrong because killing is wrong. An objection to this is that there are some circumstances in which killing is not wrong, notably killing an aggressor in self-defence. The difference between killing in self-defence and murder is that the person killed in self-defence is not innocent. The murderer is not innocent, so killing a murderer is, in the relevant respects, like killing in self-defence, and unlike murder. So capital punishment is not necessarily wrong.

(ii)   Capital punishment risks killing the innocent

We surely have enough examples of miscarriages of justice to make us believe that execution of the innocent is a real possibility if capital punishment is used. This is a problem for retributivists, because they would believe they had done something wrong if they executed an innocent person. They would probably respond by saying that we have to make sure that our system of justice is foolproof.

Utilitarians would say that if the institution of capital punishment really did deter murderers, then the unfortunate fact that sometimes the wrong person was executed wouldn't count against the rightness of capital punishment. In order to minimise suffering, they also should aim for a justice system in which miscarriages of justice were unlikely to occur. But if they did occur, that wouldn't by itself show that capital punishment was wrong.

But one argument against capital punishment says that because it is wrong to kill an innocent person, and because there is such a risk if you use capital punishment, and because you cannot make reparation for your mistake, then capital punishment is wrong.

(iii)   Utilitarianism

There could be a utilitarian argument against the death penalty, if there were good evidence that the consequences of having the death penalty were worse than those of not having it.

(iv)   The death penalty is uncivilised

This view is presented by Reiman (1985), who starts by conceding that murderers deserve the death penalty, on the grounds that it is our right to pay someone back in kind for what they have done to others. But even though they deserve it, we should not do it, because refusing to do horrible things to people, even when they deserve it, is a mark of how civilised we are. He points out that the principle of retribution means that torturers deserve to be tortured, but that the fact that we do not torture them both 'signals the level of our civilisation and, by our example, continues the work of civilising'. The greater the number of horrible things which we put into the category of things which our level of civilisation forbids us to do the better. So if execution is especially horrible, then it too should be something which civilisation demands we don't do. Reiman concedes that if there were overwhelming evidence that the death penalty deters murderers, then it may be right to use it, but in the absence of such evidence, it is not right to do so.

This position rests on a claim that the death penalty is especially awful. You need to assess this claim. In Exercise 9, you considered a condemned man's account of preparation for execution. Do cases like this show that the death penalty is especially awful? Would its awfulness depend on the method of execution?

Further reading

Glover, J. (1977) *Causing Death and Saving Lives*, London: Penguin, chapter 18.

Honderich, T. (1976) *Punishment*, Harmondsworth: Penguin.

Mill, J.S. (1986) 'Speech in Favour of Capital Punishment' (1868), in P. Singer (ed.) *Applied Ethics*, Oxford: Oxford University Press.

Reiman. J. (1985) 'Justice, Civilisation and the Death Penalty' *Philosophy and Public Affairs*, vol. 14, no. 2.

Sorell, T. (1987) *Moral Theory and Capital Punishment*, Oxford: Blackwell.

Van den Haag, E. (1983) *The Death Penalty: a Debate*, New York and London: Plenum.

Ethics and war

Two questions need to be considered in relation to the morality of war:

Can it ever be right to engage in war (including intervention in wars between other countries or groups)?

Are there any ethical limits to the ways in which wars should be conducted?

The concept of a just war

Given that war involves violence, can it ever be right to fight a war?

Pacifism

One response – that of pacifism – would be that regardless of the reasons why you may want to fight, no matter how unjustly or cruelly you have been treated, it is wrong to go to war, because war involves killing, and killing is wrong.

But if killing in self-defence is justifiable for the individual, why should it not be justifiable for a country? The most obvious example of a just war seems to be one in which a country fights in self-defence, resisting the aggression of another state or country.

Self-defence

Is retaliation to an attack really the same as self-defence – is it really like one individual killing another in self-defence? One view that it is sufficiently like self-defence to justify war in response to aggression is presented by Walzer in *Just and Unjust Wars* where he talks about 'the legalist paradigm'.

This is the idea that the relations between states and countries can be understood as analogous to the relations between individuals. We apply the notions of crime, punishment, self-defence to individuals, and we can apply them to countries as well. We must accept the right of countries to defend themselves militarily when they are attacked. If this is what it is to engage in a just war, it follows that aggression must have occurred in order for a war to be just. The side which starts the aggression cannot be acting justly. As Walzer says, a war cannot be just on both sides.

Problems with the concept of a just war

(i)   What counts as aggression?
According to Walzer, what constitutes aggression is 'Any use of force or imminent threat of force by one state against the political sovereignty or territorial integrity of another'. This definition assumes that any country has a right to its territory, and a right to self-determination or self government.

In some cases it will be fairly clear that actions count as aggressive – e.g. armies marching over borders, shooting people who protest or resist. The problem cases will be those where a judgement has to be made about the threat of force. What constitutes a threat, and how imminent does the attack have to be in order to justify a country being the first to take military action?

Some judgement has to be made on the basis of the actions of a country and its leaders. Military preparations, verbal threats, insults might be taken as indicators, but they can't necessarily justify making a pre-emptive strike.

One example shows the difficulty of interpreting military preparations as evidence of imminent attack. During the Cold War period, Americans claimed that Russia's actions in building up nuclear arms were evidence of Russia's intention to attack, whilst at the same time insisting that their own build up of nuclear arms was solely for defensive purposes. The fact that a country is increasing its armaments does not necessarily imply that it has aggressive intentions.

It is impossible to come up with a formula for deciding in all cases which country is the aggressor. But from the fact that a particular country is the first to use military action, it does not follow that that country is the aggressor and that the country which has merely been making threats is innocent.

(ii)   Is the analogy with self-defence appropriate?

First, military aggression is not necessarily a threat to the *lives* of those attacked. e.g. one country may violate the borders of another by crossing them with armed forces, but may not kill anyone, provided there is no resistance. If it were right to kill members of the armed forces in such circumstances, this could not be because it was a case of self-defence. The justification for killing in self-defence is that those who try to kill others forfeit their own right to life if the person attacked must kill them in order to survive.

Second, the justification for killing in self-defence involves the idea that the attacker is responsible for creating a situation in which there is an inescapable choice between two lives, so that if anyone should be killed it should be the attacker. But perhaps soldiers fighting in wartime are not responsible for the situation they are in.

Norman (1995) says that the self-defence justification works if individuals literally have to fight for their lives (e.g. in confrontation with individual attackers), but then that is not because it is analogous with self-defence, but because it *is* self-defence. Most killing in wartime is more like retaliation or pre-emptive strike than self-defence.

(iii)   Can intervention be justified?

There are two kinds of circumstance in which intervention may be considered: first, going to the assistance of a country which has been attacked, by taking military action against the aggressor; second, taking military action inside a country in which there is civil war or revolution.

In the first kind of case, if the country which has been attacked has a right to self-defence, then why shouldn't it be right for others to assist them in their defence? Would we accept that in cases of self-defence in general?

An example of the second kind of case is provided by the recent conflict in Bosnia. Some politicians said that Britain should not intervene in Bosnia because intervention would not achieve the aim of ending massacre. But supposing intervention did have good consequences, would it be right to intervene?

If other countries had taken military action on Bosnian territory, or tried to impose a political solution by threat of force, then they would have been intervening in the domestic affairs of what was formerly Yugoslavia. Walzer sets out John Stuart Mill's position on intervention, which says that states are to be treated as self-determining, even if their citizens don't have political freedom. A state can't be self-determining if someone else comes in and imposes a solution. So the citizens have to be left to conduct their struggle without assistance from outside.

There are two problems with this. Not only does it seem extremely harsh to say that no matter what is happening to the inhabitants of a country, no-one should go to their assistance, but also it seems to be much too simplistic a model to apply to something like the conflict in the former Yugoslavia. Is a state to be defined by the boundaries of the territory it occupies, or by the ethnic group to which its members belong, or what? The result of failing to intervene could be that some ethnic groups may be wiped out.

The conduct of a just war

If we accept that there can be such a thing as a just war, it doesn't follow that there are no moral restrictions on the kinds of things one may do in a war.

Absolute prohibition on the killing of non-combatants

This is a view that there are absolute restrictions on the character of the violence which it is morally acceptable to use. For example, the Geneva Convention says:

> In order to ensure respect for and protection of the civilian population and civilian objects, the Parties to the conflict shall at all times distinguish between the civilian population and combatants and between civilian objects and military objectives and accordingly shall direct their operations only against military objectives..The civilian population   as such, as well as individual citizens, shall not be the object of attack.

Deliberate killing of non-combatants is not morally acceptable, even if it is going to have good consequences in the long run, but this is often ignored (the allied bombings of German cities in World War Two, and dropping atom bombs on Hiroshima and Nagasaki are examples where innocent civilians were deliberately killed).

Unlike a utilitarian view, this absolutist position is interested in the

character of the individual's action, not in the final results. So it would forbid the killing of innocent people, even if by killing some innocent people you might believe that you are going to reduce the number of deaths in the long run (the kind of justification sometimes given for Hiroshima).
Problems:

(i)   Fuzzy distinctions
The position relies on distinctions between combatants and non-combatants, and between military and non-military targets. If combatants means members of the armed forces, it includes cooks, drivers, as well as people who use weapons, and it excludes workers in munitions factories and politicians (who might be equally, or more, 'responsible' for deaths).

Is a bridge which has strategic importance, but is regularly used by civilians a military or a non-military target? Or an air-raid shelter used by both civilians and military?

(ii)   Why is it morally acceptable to kill a combatant, but not to kill a non-combatant?
Is it because non-combatants are innocent? If innocent means 'not guilty', why should we think that soldiers who are fighting for a just cause are guilty? Or does innocent mean 'harmless', as opposed to harming?

(iii)   Can the idea of self-defence justify the killing of soldiers?
If so, it would be morally acceptable to kill only those who pose a direct threat to one's life. This would rule out, for example, surprise attacks on troops.

(iv)   Killing civilians is using them as a mere means
This Kantian view is put forward by Nagel (1972). Can it really defend a moral distinction between killing soldiers and killing civilians? Why should we think that when soldiers are killed, they are not being used as a mere means?

The doctrine of double effect as a justification for civilian deaths

The doctrine of double effect is sometimes applied to the bombing of military targets in which civilians might be killed (e.g. bombing munitions factories).

The doctrine says: it is sometimes permissible knowingly to bring about as a side effect of one's actions something which it would be impermissible to bring about deliberately.

This permits some civilian deaths to be brought about as a result of bombing military targets, provided the intention is merely to destroy the military target. (See our discussion of problems with this doctrine in Chapter 5.)

Utilitarian view

Just war and intervention

Utilitarians must consider the consequences of going to war, or of intervening in a war. Armed combat might bring about the best result, so utilitarians could believe that some wars and some interventions were justified. Strictly speaking, of course, utilitarians should consider the welfare of everyone involved, and not just the welfare of their own country. Because results are difficult to predict, it is sometimes suggested that utilitarians could consistently take a pacifist position. This would be what Glover calls contingent pacifism (Glover, 1990: 258).

Contingent pacifism

The pacifism of the utilitarian is contingent upon what is believed to be the result of not taking a pacifist line. It is a view that the consequences of not going to war will never be as bad as the war itself would be. Or it might involve the view that even if in a particular case the results would be better if one went to war, it is still better to have a pacifist policy, because the policy of never resorting to military force will do less harm in the long run.

There is a further argument in favour of contingent pacifism – the idea that in refusing to fight we set an example. The more often countries indicate that they will not use violence as a means of settling disputes, the more likely it is that peaceful means of settlement of disputes becomes the norm.

Conduct of war

There is nothing in the utilitarian principle itself which rules out what might seem to be morally objectionable means of achieving our ends. For example, if you think you can end a war quickly by directly bombing civilians, then utilitarianism may be able to justify dropping the bombs. There is some disagreement on such matters amongst utilitarians. Glover, for example, suggests that it is consistent for utilitarians to say that it will be for the best if countries act as if there were an absolute prohibition on killing innocent civilians, even though the utilitarian principle itself doesn't rule out such killing, and even though in some cases you could save more lives by killing some innocent civilians.

Utilitarianism does not imply that 'anything goes' in warfare. Actions have to be done for the sake of some good outcome, so any harmful actions of soldiers which don't contribute to the aim of speedy victory wouldn't be morally acceptable (e.g. reprisals against captives, rape and murder of civilians). Also, the good aimed at has to outweigh the harm which is inflicted, so any killing in warfare, so far as utilitarianism is concerned, must be necessary for a military objective, and must not be disproportionate to the goal which is achieved.

Further reading

Cohen, M., Nagel, T. and Scanlon, T. (eds) (1974) *War and Moral Responsibility*, Princeton, NJ and London: Princeton University Press.

Glover, J. (1977) *Causing Death and Saving Lives*, London: Penguin, chapter 19.

Nagel, T. (1972) 'War and Massacre' in *Philosophy and Public Affairs*, vol. 1, no. 2, Winter 1972.

Norman, R. (1995) *Ethics, Killing and War*, Cambridge: Cambridge University Press.

Walzer, M. (1980) *Just and Unjust Wars*, Harmondsworth: Penguin.

Bibliography

Aitken, W. and LaFollette, H. (1977) (eds) *World Hunger and Moral Obligation*, Englewood Cliffs, NJ: Prentice Hall.

Attfield, R. (1983) *The Ethics of Environmental Concern*, Oxford: Blackwell.

Beauchamp, T.L. and Childress, J.F. (1983) *Principles of Biomedical Ethics*, New York and Oxford: Oxford University Press.

Campbell, R. and Collinson, D. (1988) *Ending Lives*, Oxford: Blackwell.

Clarke, S. (1984) *The Moral Status of Animals*, Oxford: Clarendon Press.

Cohen, M., Nagel, T. and Scanlon, T. (eds) (1974) *War and Moral Responsibility*, Princeton, NJ and London: Princeton University Press.

Dworkin, R. (1993) *Life's Dominion*, London: Harper-Collins.

Fisher, A.E. (1988) *The Logic of Real Arguments*, Cambridge: Cambridge University Press.

Fisher, A.E. and Scriven, M. (1997) *Critical Thinking: Defining and Assessing It*, California: Edge Press, and Norwich, UK: Centre for Research in Critical Thinking.

Foot, P. (1977) 'Euthanasia', *Philosophy and Public Affairs*, vol. 6, no. 2.

Glover, J. (1990) *Causing Death and Saving Lives*, London: Penguin.

Govier, T. (1985) *A Practical Study of Argument*, Belmont, CA: Wadsworth.

Harris J. (1985) *The Value of Life*, London: Routledge & Kegan Paul.

Honderich, T. (1976) *Punishment*, Harmondsworth: Penguin.

Hume, D. (1961) 'Enquiry Concerning the Principles of Morals' in L.A. Selby-Bigge (ed) *Enquiries*, Oxford: Clarendon Press.

—— (1966) *A Treatise of Human Nature*, Book III of *Morals*, London: Dent; New York, Dutton; Everyman's Library.

Hursthouse, R. (1987) *Beginning Lives*, Oxford: Blackwell.

LaFollette, H. and Shanks, N. (1996) *Brute Science*, London and New York: Routledge.

Leopold, A. (1966) *A Sand County Almanac*, New York: Oxford University Press.

Midgley, M. (1983) *Animals and Why They Matter*, Harmondsworth: Penguin.

Mill, J. S. (1863) *Utilitarianism* in M. Warnock (ed) (1962) *Utilitarianism*, Great Britain: Collins/Fontana.

—— (1986) 'Speech in Favour of Capital Punishment' (1868), in P. Singer (ed.) *Applied Ethics*, Oxford: Oxford University Press.

Nagel, T. (1972) 'War and Massacre' in *Philosophy and Public Affairs*, vol. 1, no. 2, Winter 1972.

Norman, R. (1995) *Ethics, Killing and War*, Cambridge: Cambridge University Press.

O'Neill, O. (1986) *Faces of Hunger*, London: Allen & Unwin.

Paton, H.J. (1948) *The Moral Law*, London, New York, Melbourne, Sydney, Cape Town: Hutchinson's University Library.

Paul, R. (1990) *Critical Thinking*, Center for Critical Thinking and Moral Critique: Sonoma State University, Rohnert Park, CA.

Rachels, J. (1986) 'Active and Passive Euthanasia', in P. Singer (ed.) *Applied Ethics*, Oxford: Oxford University Press.

—— (1993) *The Elements of Moral Philosophy*, McGraw-Hill.

Rawls, J. (1971) *A Theory of Justice*, Cambridge: Harvard University Press.

Regan, T. and Singer, P. (1976) *Animal Rights and Human Obligations*, Englewood Cliffs and London: Prentice Hall.

Regan, T. (ed) (1980) *Matters of Life and Death*, New York: Random House.

Reiman. J. (1985) 'Justice, Civilisation and the Death Penalty', *Philosophy and Public Affairs*, vol. 14, no. 2.

Siegel, H. (1988) *Educating Reason*, New York and London: Routledge.

Singer, P. (1973) 'Animal Liberation', in *The New York Review of Books*, 5 April 1973.

Singer, P. (ed) (1986a) *Applied Ethics*, Oxford: Oxford University Press.

Singer, P. (1986b) 'All Animals are Equal', in P. Singer (ed.) *Applied Ethics*, Oxford: Oxford University Press.

—— (1993) *Practical Ethics*, 2nd edn, Cambridge: Cambridge University Press.

Sorell, T. (1987) *Moral Theory and Capital Punishment*, Oxford: Blackwell.

Swartz, R. and Parks, S. (1992) *Infusing Critical and Creative Thinking into Content Instruction*, Pacific Grove, CA: Critical Thinking Press and Software.

Thomson, A. (1996) *Critical Reasoning – A Practical Introduction*, London: Routledge.

Thomson, J.J. (1971) 'A Defence of Abortion', *Philosophy and Public Affairs* (Fall 1971): 48–53.

Tooley, M. (1986) 'Abortion and Infanticide', in P. Singer (ed.) *Applied Ethics*, Oxford: Oxford University Press.

Van den Haag, E. (1983) *The Death Penalty: a Debate*, New York and London: Plenum.

Waldron, J. (1984) *Theories of Rights*, Oxford: Oxford University Press.

Walzer, M. (1980) *Just and Unjust Wars*, Harmondsworth: Penguin.

Warburton, N. (1996) *Thinking from A to Z*, London: Routledge.

Index

211